No Deed Greater Than A Word

A New Approach To Biblical Preaching

William H. Shepherd, Jr.

CSS Publishing Company, Inc., Lima, Ohio

NO DEED GREATER THAN A WORD

Copyright © 1998 by
CSS Publishing Company, Inc.
Lima, Ohio

All rights reserved. No part of this publication may be reproduced in any manner whatsoever without the prior permission of the publisher, except in the case of brief quotations embodied in critical articles and reviews. Inquiries should be addressed to: Permissions, CSS Publishing Company, Inc., P.O. Box 4503, Lima, Ohio 45802-4503.

Scripture quotations except as noted are from the *New Revised Standard Version of the Bible*, copyright 1989 by the Division of Christian Education of the National Council of the Churches of Christ in the USA. Used by permission.

Library of Congress Cataloging-in-Publication Data

Shepherd, William H. (William Henry), 1957-
   No deed greater than a word : a new approach to biblical preaching / William H. Shepherd, Jr.
     p.   cm.
   Includes bibliographical reference.
   ISBN 0-7880-1180-4 (pbk.)
   1. Preaching. I. Title.
BV4211.2.S494   1997
251—dc21   97-28495
                                                                                                CIP

ISBN 0-7880-1180-4   PRINTED IN U.S.A.

To Luke and Fred

Table of Contents

Preface	7
Chapter 1: No Deed Greater Than A Word	11
Speech That Acts	15
The Creative Word	18
News And Information	24
The Word, Living And Active	28
Conclusion	32
Chapter 2: Reading The Readers	35
Listening Readers	36
Interpretive Communities And Congregations	42
Congregations As Implied Readers	50
Establishing An Interpretive Community	55
Conclusion	58
Chapter 3: Reading The Text	61
Reading Presuppositions	63
Three Presuppositions:	
Religion Thinks, Feels, Or Does	65
The Bible And "Religion Thinks"	67
The Bible And "Religion Feels"	70
The Bible And "Religion Does"	76
Reading Critically	78
Reading Otherness	82
Divine And Human Otherness	83
Otherness And The Biblical Text	87
Reading Canonically	92
Conclusion	97

Chapter 4: Reading To The Congregation   101
Orality: The Text In Time   105
Gaps: Holes In The Sermon   109
Form   112
   Orality, Gaps, And Form   114
   The Bible And Form   117
Language   119
   Orality, Gaps, And Language   120
   Language Concrete And Vivid   123
   Leading With The Heart, Leading With The Head:
      Story In The Sermon   126
   On Metaphor   130
   The Bible And Oral Language   133
Conclusion   134

Chapter 5: Reading The Sermon   137
Preaching Bible vs. Preaching Gospel   138
   A Critique Of Biblical Preaching: Edward Farley   138
   Beyond The Bridge Paradigm: A Response To Farley   141
Grace And The Interpretive Community   147
Conclusion: Preaching Grace   152

Preface

This book is written for preachers who suspect that the way they were taught to preach (and, for the most part, are still being taught to preach) simply does not work. Some of them will have spent long hard hours in the study doing all the proper steps of biblical exegesis, only to find their congregations squirming and listless under the results. Others will have, with some guilt feelings, abandoned any attempt to be biblical, except in the broadest sense, in favor of being interesting. Most, I suppose, make do with a brief skimming of one or two popular sermon aids before launching into the real business of getting the sermon down on paper. The time has passed when homileticians could merely exhort their former students to recover older and better interpretive habits; the habits were lost because they were not helpful. There is something wrong here, but the fault is systemic, not personal. The problem is with the underlying conception of the pulpit.

I have tried to rethink the sermon in light of several years of interdisciplinary work in literary criticism, theology, and biblical studies. Under the overarching rubric of "reading," I argue that preaching is reading in the widest sense of that term: the reading of texts within and for an interpretive community, which results in a new understanding of the world and our place in it. Throughout, my concern is to enable the preacher to bring the Bible to life in the sermon in all its literary, historical, and religious dimensions. Literary theory, which began dripping into biblical studies a few years ago and now has grown into a flood, has taught us that reading canonical texts requires reading their readers also — that is, the preacher must understand the listeners as well as the message — and that this is a communal process, even for the preacher sitting alone in the study. The preacher who reads thus creates a new text, the sermon itself, which in turn is read by preacher and congregation. The sermon creates a new world, and this world itself becomes and is a text of sorts, interpreted and reinterpreted by preacher and congregation in the ongoing task of preaching, thus ever becoming new.

So this is not so much a how-to book, but a how-to-think-about-it book. It is a plain language translation of contemporary literary and theological concepts, with clear application to preaching. While it is not a textbook on preaching, it does contain many examples of how I would do it, based on what I have learned. Theory cannot be divorced from practice, especially in the pulpit, and I have tried to put names and faces on every theoretical abstraction.

Some will note my obvious debt to scholarly trends that in the literary world are called postmodern, in biblical studies, postcritical, and in systematic theology, postliberal. These labels may be helpful to some of my readers, but I have not made use of them in what follows, being hesitant to label myself purely in terms of what preceded me. I have concentrated on the argument rather than its appellation. Those who wish to follow the broader implications of these trends may begin with the works mentioned in the endnotes.

Thanks to those who read and evaluated the early drafts of this work, especially Iris Burnell, Barry Evans, Geoffrey Hoare, Nancy Shepherd, and Norman Runnion. Others who contributed to its production in various ways include Brian and Judith Jones, Gail O'Day, and Mac Paterson. Many of my former students, too many to name or even recall, will recognize (and, I hope, be glad to see) bits and pieces of their work in my illustrations. Thanks also to the people of St. George's Episcopal Church in Pennsville, New Jersey, who listened patiently to my own preaching during the writing of this book.

This book is dedicated to two people whose thoughts I sometimes have trouble distinguishing from my own. I owe much of my thinking about preaching to Fred Craddock, whose name appears often in this text, usually when I have nothing to say that he has not already said better. Even when I have gone ahead and said it, I can't help but hear Fred's voice there. In particular, I owe to Fred the aphorism that suggests the title of this book and the first chapter: "There is no deed greater than a word."

Luke Johnson has contributed not so much particular words but a way of thinking about theology, biblical studies, and life itself. Much of what I have done here is far from original, because it was his first. I hope that he will not be displeased with the use to which I have put it, and be as honored to have me as a student as I am to have him as teacher and friend.

Chapter 1

No Deed Greater Than A Word

Suppose I say the word "cat." What comes to mind? If you are like most people I've met, you will immediately imagine a furry, whiskery face — and it will be purring fuzzily under your outstretched hand, or digging up your garden with its claws, depending on your attitude towards the house cats in your neighborhood. Whether you are comforted or annoyed by the image, you probably picture the same kind of cat that I picture: four legs, whiskers, a tail, named Tom or Tabby or Felix. The picture is the same no matter how we feel about it. The word "cat" has a clear counterpart in our everyday world; here is a clear, one-to-one relationship between word and reality. For most people, this is exactly how words work: you use a word to refer to one specific thing that exists in a real, tangible world.

Common sense and tradition tell us that words reflect reality. But is language really so simple? Think again about the seemingly transparent meaning of the word "cat." Must it refer to the house cat we thought of when we first heard the word? What if I say the word "cat" while standing before a cage in the zoo, or by the shore of the lake, or watching an Alfred Hitchcock movie? You will, of course, think in succession of a lion, a sailboat, and Cary Grant scuttling across the rooftops. If language merely reflects reality, how can one three-letter word do so much work, in effect reflecting so many realities? And what will you think of if I stand in the pulpit and say the words, "Kingdom of God" — what reality, if any, will that phrase conjure in your mind?

Words can and do reflect reality, but even as they do, they suggest possibilities beyond our tempting initial supposition that there is a one-to-one correspondence between any given word and a particular reality. Words can mean many things; they can mean nothing. They can refer to hopes and dreams as well as realities. Words can have so many meanings that it may be hard to figure out at first what exactly words do mean, sometimes even when you have uttered them yourself.

The theory that words merely reflect reality makes one thing easy: the denigration of words. Words become a pale imitation of the real thing, an unworthy substitute for concrete reality. "I want action, not words." "Talk is cheap." There is a widespread prejudice against words for words' sake. Many feel that what counts in this world is not what you say but what you do. Under this pragmatic prejudice, the spoken word does not count for much. Words, after all, are just containers of meaning, not the thing itself.

However, not all talk is cheap. "The physicists have known sin," said physicist Robert Oppenheimer, reflecting on his work in the Manhattan Project, the wartime quest for the atomic bomb. The words have their obvious meaning, expressing the regret of one who helped open Pandora's box. Some have noticed, in addition, the slight underlying sexual overtones, in light of the biblical use of the verb "to know," not to mention the connotation of "sin" in popular culture. Oppenheimer and his colleagues in fact frequently used the language of sexuality to describe their work. Natural science, going back as far as the scientific architects Francis Bacon and Robert Boyle, has often made use of a metaphor that pictures reason as male, reasonable, and dominating, and nature as female, mysterious, and uncontrolled; this metaphor was given tangible expression in a statue at the medical school of the University of Paris of a bare-breasted young woman removing her veil, with the inscription, "Nature unveils herself before Science." In the case of atomic secrets, where Nature was not so willing to disrobe, she had to be controlled — by violence if need be. Oppenheimer and the physicists working with him described their absorbing, compulsive work in violently sexual terms. For example, they claimed to have "penetrated one of Nature's innermost secrets." The "father of atomic physics," Ernest Rutherford, was said to have the word "attack" often on his lips. Teaching and research were described as "insemination." The result of their work was parentage, the production of a "baby" — the Bomb.[1]

My point is not morality but the relation of word and deed. Let the preacher consider the metaphor, along with its users. Here were scientists, all male, exploring the most destructive force known to humanity. Their language described their work in sexual terms, and not with sentiments of love, but in terms of rape. The inherent violence of their goal was matched by their language — if Germany, and later Japan, were to be taken by force, Nature must first be conquered. The language is striking, given the setting, and one may wonder whether the situation produced the language, or vice-versa. What was the relationship between their words and deeds?

An obvious and easy answer is that the language of sexual violence reflected the underlying anxiety of wartime — violent times produce violent language. One can make a case that the language used by the scientists helped further the project. The violent language fueled the inherently violent work, and that the language was sexual makes the results more poignant, in light of what the wartime physicists' offspring could do, and may yet still do, to Mother Earth. Sticks and stones can break your bones, but in this case, words gave birth to the destroyer of worlds.

I suggest, in line with a growing trend in philosophy, literary criticism, and linguistics, that language can create reality as much as reflect it. Words are not merely passive, meaning-toting buckets to be spilled out when the time comes. Words can change things. Like sticks and stones, they can do good or ill. They can move armies or mobilize volunteers. They are more than pale reflections of something else. Words, far from being, as Joseph Conrad put it, "the great foes of reality,"[2] are what make reality real. There is no deed greater than a word.

Politicians have always known this, in a crude sort of way — a missile named "Peacemaker" has a better chance of making it through Congress and becoming a reality than one named, say, "Warmonger." When George Bush continually referred to Saddam Hussein and Hitler in the same breath, he was trying to rally his audience by rubbing an old conflict against a new one, hoping the just, patriotic smell of the fight against Nazism would rub off. In portraying Hussein as Hitler, Bush did not so much reflect reality — as the brief Gulf War showed, Iraq was not nearly as powerful a state as Nazi Germany had been — as create it: the carefully chosen words produced the desired effect, a consensus that this new tyrant must be stopped. As the old saw goes, if you say it long enough, you start believing it.

Even when we can't quite put our finger on it, we sense that to change the words is to change the reality. This is especially true in the life of a congregation. In the late 1940s, when the infant *Revised Standard Version* was first issued, some church members held ritual burnings of the new Bible translation. Even now there are those who long for the stately cadences of the old translation; I once attended a church where a woman ran for a lay leadership position on the platform that she would work to restore the *King James Version* to Sunday worship — and she won! In my denomination, the Episcopal Church, there is a group called the Prayer Book Society devoted to the restoration of the Elizabethan language of the old 1928 *Book of Common Prayer*; anyone who has ever had a conversation with a member of this society knows how ardent is their belief that the new words have changed the old ways too much, and none for the better. Any change in Sunday liturgy may produce some dissent, but a feminist liturgy of milk-and-honey rituals and prayers to Sophia is likely to evoke a maelstrom. This is not mere resistance to change for its own sake, but the gut feeling of the faithful that to change the words is somehow to change the reality. That feeling is correct: *The Revised Standard Version* made the Bible more readable, the 1979 Prayer Book made worship more accessible, and prayers to Sophia allow worshipers to envision God and the world in a different way — if you are not trying to change the reality, why change the language?

The power of language to influence our perception of the world is illustrated in this exchange between two preachers on the subject of gender-inclusive language:

"I know," says one, "that when the Bible or the hymnal says 'men,' it means 'everyone.'"

"Okay," says the other, "name the three men who have most influenced your life."

"My father, my brother, and my son."

"Why no women on your list, if they are included when I say 'men'?"

Even when we want to hear "men" as "all," we may not really be able to. The ingrained power of language suggests a reality that our conscious minds reject.

One smart preacher I know proves the point quite simply. He asks his audience to stand up. They stand up. He asks them to turn and face the rear of the room. They turn and face the rear of the room. He asks them to turn again to the front. They turn. He asks them to sit. They sit. Then he grins at them and says, "Why did you do that? Just because I told you so? Does anyone here now doubt the power of the spoken word?"

Speech That Acts

Of course anyone who has been a pastor for longer than six months knows that real change is not effected so easily as a simple command to stand and face the rear of the room; if it were so, our stewardship campaigns would be a lot easier. When I say that language creates reality, I do not mean anything so simplistic as, "When you tell people to do something, they will do it." What I mean is that in many kinds of communications, when a speaker uses words, those words are not merely passive containers of meaning. Rather, those words do something. They are *performative*.

The notion that words can be "performative" stems from the English philosopher J. L. Austin, the founder of what is known as "speech act theory." In his appropriately and playfully titled *How to Do Things with Words*, Austin criticized the longstanding philosophical theory that language consisted mostly of true or false utterances about the world.[3] Some words do seem to report, rightly or wrongly, on external affairs; these utterances Austin called "constative." But not all of our words, Austin noted, describe some reality outside themselves. Words can be "performative" when they are meant to get something done. Performative utterances are verbal actions: "I pronounce you husband and wife," or "I hereby arrest you in the name of the law," or "I promise to uphold and defend the Constitution of the United States." Performative language comes in two basic forms.[4] Some performative utterances have an active function: the words do something in the very act of saying something. "I take you to be my wedded husband" actually does what it says, as does almost any statement of promise, threat, affirmation, intimidation, or reassurance. The other kind of performative utterance, in contrast, aims to convince or persuade — to have a certain effect on the hearer. The television ad that touts the product as "new" and "free" (two of the most powerful words in the English language) aims for a simple performative effect: compel the viewer to go out and buy the product.

In the church we use language that does more than reflect truth or error about reality — language that is performative — every day. In some theological traditions "I accept Jesus Christ as my Savior" has a performative effect of the first kind; for all intents and purposes it accomplishes conversion (humanly speaking). In other traditions "I baptize you in the name of the Father, the Son, and the Holy Spirit" has the same effect. Performative utterances of the second kind, intended to please, move, or persuade, abound in ecclesiastic circles. A typical stewardship speech will be filled with performative acts, as the speaker will urge, cajole, and exhort the hearers to fill out their pledge cards in a spirit of generosity. The second kind of performative utterances, intended to convince or persuade, is found particularly in sermons, though all too often the desired effects are at variance with the results; the preacher who tells people what to do usually produces unintended action: yawns, shuffling, and squirming. People naturally resist an all-out assault on their freedom to think and act; tell them not to think of elephants, and their minds will be filled with images of Barnum and Bailey, or Dumbo and his mother. To speak the performative word, and to be effective in speaking that word, are two different things. But the first step is to recognize how much of our speech is performative. Austin himself came to the conclusion that even constative, "true or false" utterances, while ostensibly merely reflections of reality, were really performances: they perform the act of asserting something.

Certainly the preacher will need to make statements (presumably true ones) about reality. Sometimes people use language simply to convey information: "The number you have dialed has been changed. The new number is...." All sermons have information, and information is best conveyed in the no-nonsense style of a good news reporter. Consider this section from one of my own sermons:

> *Pentecost is the day the Church celebrates gifts, especially the gift of new life. Pentecost is traditionally the last day of the Easter season, the fiftieth day after Christ broke out of the tomb. It was originally a Jewish harvest feast, a time when Jews from all the world traveled to Jerusalem to celebrate. As the story goes in Acts, it was on this feast day of Pentecost that the Holy Spirit came on the disciples and they began to witness to the good news of new life in Jesus.*

The writing is straightforward, if a little dull. The pulse does not quicken, but it is not meant to. The paragraph merely communicates information; nothing more is required of it.

But sometimes words do more than just inform: they create an experience of some sort:

> *Once upon a midnight dreary, while I pondered, weak and weary,*
> *Over many a quaint and curious volume of forgotten lore —*
> *While I nodded, nearly napping, suddenly there came a tapping,*
> *As of someone gently rapping, rapping at my chamber door.*
> *" 'Tis some visitor," I muttered, "tapping at my chamber door —*
> *Only this and nothing more."*

How do you feel now? Most of us, by the end of the first stanza of Poe's "The Raven," have moved to a dark, drowsy, slightly bookish place, and many will become nostalgic for the fifth grade. Certainly we are not where we were when the recorded voice of the operator was telling us the new number. The language is performative and does what it says — it creates a certain experience. It cannot be reduced to mere information.

In my Pentecost sermon quoted above, I wanted the congregation to view their own lives as a gift. I wrote a few lines and concluded,

> *Can you really say that your life is not a gift? Can you believe that the talents and skills and resources that get you through day by day are all, entirely, without question your own? I don't think so.*

Clear enough, but it seemed flat; I could picture them nodding their heads, in fatigue if not in agreement. What was lacking was the language that would make it so — words that would wake them up and remind them vividly of their interdependence, and thus of their status as dependent beings before a Creator. I added a few lines as follows:

> *Can you really say that your life is not a gift? Can you believe that the talents and skills and resources that get you through day by day are all, entirely, without question your own? I don't think so. But if you do, maybe you've forgotten the egg on your breakfast plate — and the grocer who sold you that egg, the stock boy who put the egg carton on the shelf, the trucker who brought the eggs from the dairy, the farmer who sold the eggs to the dairy, the hen who laid the egg, and the rooster who got the hen pregnant in the first place. No one is an island, or even a peninsula.*

Effective preaching doesn't just say it is so, it creates the experience of it being so.

The Creative Word

Few would deny that the language of the sermon is intended to be performative — moving, persuading, or convincing. The popular image of the sermon is as a lecture that tells people what to do. Certainly the preacher who wishes to move or persuade a congregation can learn the most effective kinds of rhetoric for that purpose. But I am not primarily interested in the purely rhetorical side of how things are done with words according to Austin. Rhetorical tricks can be learned anywhere and everywhere. I would like to consider the extent to which the sermon can be considered a performative utterance of the first kind. That is, does the sermon in and of itself do something? If Austin is right, there is a possibility that the sermon might not only convey information or change the emotional state of the hearers, but might actually create reality.

A preacher might say, "We're all mortal," and would win a vote of confidence for conveying an accurate and widely-accepted bit of information. A preacher who aims at getting the congregation to experience a bit of mortality might say,

> *We know that any time, without warning, just like that, a runaway car, a stray gene or virus, any number of accidents or crimes or just plain bad luck can end what began with the crying of a red-faced little mammal, still tied by a cord to mother.*

Yet another preacher, in another pastoral situation, or perhaps at the end of a story, might say, "We held hands and prayed at the bedside when Jimmy died last night," and in so saying, create the Church.

If preaching can create reality, the preacher must ask what sort of reality he or she is interested in creating. The answer is obvious: preaching creates the Church. But it does not do so by telling church members to shape up, or by informing people of certain facts that are helpful for pewsitters to know. Preaching shapes the world of its listeners by providing experiences, which produce a new community called the Church. The preacher uses words to shape a new world. The hearers over time become the Church envisaged by the preacher. The sermon is a world.

Again, I speak in accord with a strong interdisciplinary trend. There is a sizeable body of scholarship in anthropology, sociology, philosophy, history, religious studies, and literary criticism that suggests that language, particularly religious language, creates and enables reality. Yale theologian George Lindbeck has made the most explicit theological use of this insight.[5] Lindbeck, drawing primarily on the philosopher of language Ludwig Wittgenstein and the sociologist Clifford Geertz, believes that a religion provides a set of symbols and rules for making sense out of life; thus a religion is like a language, with words (symbols that convey meaning) and grammar (rules for putting words together), or a culture, with its symbolic stories and expected behavior (thus Lindbeck dubs his approach "cultural-linguistic"; in this book I will call it "Religion Does"). Religions are "comprehensive interpretive schemes,"[6] which provide a structure for one's self-understanding and give shape to all human experience:

> *A religion can be viewed as a kind of cultural and/or linguistic framework or medium that shapes the entirety of life and thought ... It is similar to an idiom that makes possible the description of realities, the formulation of beliefs, and the experiencing of inner attitudes, feelings, and sentiments.*[7]

As a religion, then, Christianity can be understood as a culture or a language; to function within it, we must learn the society's stories and its ritual behavior — its vocabulary and grammar. Christian thought enables the practice of Christianity. "Just as an individual becomes human by learning a language, so he or she begins to become a new creature through hearing and interiorizing the language that speaks of Christ."[8]

Lindbeck contrasts his approach with two other long-dominant ways of thinking theologically. The first and oldest is the common-sense notion that theological statements are simply propositions about reality (thus Lindbeck dubs this position "propositionalism"; I call it "Religion Thinks"). In this view, to speak theologically is simply to make statements about reality, in the spirit of "God said it, I believe it, that settles it." Theological statements, like scientific or mathematical statements, can be either true or false, and true religion can be found only where true beliefs are held; understanding leads to faith, or perhaps is itself faith.

The second way of theological thinking, according to Lindbeck, has been one dominant in the modern age, which stems from the work of nineteenth century theologian Friedrich Schleiermacher. Schleiermacher spoke of the religious impluse as "the feeling of absolute dependence." For Schleiermacher, theology is born in the expression of religious feelings (Lindbeck calls this position "experiential-expressivism"; I call it "Religion Feels"). In this case, what comes first is the chicken, not the egg — one has a religious experience and then seeks to explain it. Faith comes first, then understanding. Where propositionalism appeals to the common-sense notion that somebody's got to be right and that makes the others wrong, experiential-expressivism appeals to the democratic impulse: we all have an experience of God but express it differently. Thus all religions can be true insofar as they are based on true religious experiences.

I will return later to the distinctions Lindbeck makes between propositionalism, experiential-expressivism, and his own cultural-linguistic model; for now it may be helpful to note that Lindbeck, long involved in interdenominational Christian discussion, writes in search of a model for ecumenical theology. Consistent propositionalism (or "Religion Thinks"), of course, allows for no such discussion, nor for any doctrinal change other than capitulation to the other side; if I am right, then you are wrong, now and always. Modern theologians have found experiential-expressivism (or "Religion Feels") a more congenial home, but as Lindbeck notes, the idea that we all are saying the same thing and having the same experience of God stretches to the breaking point when we consider the very real differences between, say, Roman Catholicism and the Wesleyan holiness tradition, or between Christianity and Buddhism.[9]

In contrast with this long-dominant theory of religion that sees religious experience as producing theological thought, Lindbeck believes that it is for the most part the other way around: "Religion Does" in the sense that it permits and even creates religious experience. Our experiences as human beings are molded by cultural and linguistic norms, and inner religious experiences are no different. Like Helen Keller, who felt water gushing over her right hand thousands of times before she could name it with the symbols etched into the palm of her left hand, we cannot have a religious experience until we have religious language; reality requires symbols to make it comprehensible. To become religious is to become skilled in a particular religious system. If Christians display exemplary love, it is not because they were loving people who found their way into the church, but because the example of Christ, and his command to "love one another as I have loved you," enabled them to imagine and enact a new reality. If they proclaim the good news of God in Christ with boldness, they are no doubt shaped by the example of Peter and Paul in Acts. Attitudes of charity, compassion, humility, and joy do not first exist and then find expression in stories about a woman with only two mites, an apostle named Barnabas, and an ex-demoniac now clothed and in his right mind; the stories come first, then the attitudes.

> *To become religious — no less than to become culturally or linguistically competent — is to interiorize a set of skills by practice and training. One learns how to feel, act, and think in conformity with a religious tradition that is, in its inner structure, far richer and more subtle than can be explicitly articulated. The primary knowledge is not about the religion, nor that the religion teaches such and such, but rather how to be religious in such and such ways.*[10]

Christian behavior is shaped and enabled by the stories, teachings, and rituals of the Church.

The interaction between language and experience is not a one-way street, of course; at times a new experience will produce new language, as when the first disciples, convinced that Jesus was alive, undertook a massive re-interpretation of the traditional symbolic world of Judaism. But the existence of that symbolic world and their lengthy dip into it provided the basis of their new endeavor. The symbolic world of Torah was the raw material for their reorganization of the tradition; they would not have created a religion that looked like Buddhism.

Scripture, for Lindbeck, plays a formative role in the making of a Christian. Scripture is the primary source of the language, ideas, and stories that form Christian consciousness. And for Lindbeck, it is not, as one often hears, that Christians find their stories in the Bible, but rather the other way around; the biblical stories change the Christians' perceptions of life around them. Bible-reading Christians look up from the Book to see the world with new eyes.

> *They make the story of the Bible their story. The cross is not to be viewed as a figurative representation of suffering nor the messianic kingdom as a symbol for hope in the future; rather, suffering should be cruciform, and hopes for the future messianic ... It is the text, so to speak, which absorbs the world, rather than the world the text.*[11]

This all-absorbing scriptural text engulfs the lives of believers, making all things new:

> *For those who are steeped in them [the scriptures], no world is more real than the ones they create. A scriptural world is thus able to absorb the universe. It supplies the interpretive framework within which believers seek to live their lives and understand reality.*[12]

Scripture is the lens through which Christians see the world; no matter how the world changes, the lens remains the same.

Yet it is precisely because the world changes that we need the sermon. To extend the metaphor, the lens sometimes needs to be cleaned, polished, and refocused, and that is the job of the sermon. Lindbeck sees the sermon as performing primarily a catechetical function.[13] He does not mean by this that the sermon will be limited to dry, bare-bones exposition of doctrine, or a routine reiteration of an official statement of faith. A sermon in Lindbeck's view seeks to instill the language and rituals of the Christian faith by using the language of scripture. The preacher will not begin, "What Jesus meant to say in the parable of the sower was ..." but instead will weave the parable of the sower in and out of modern life. This kind of preaching cannot be summed up in a "sermon in a sentence" (though every sermon needs such a sentence to give it unity). A simple declarative sentence cannot capture what happens when a congregation is given extensive exposure to Christian scripture in the sermon. The thoughts, words, and images of the biblical writers will, over time, take over and put modern life at their feet.

In summary, Lindbeck's work offers a neat and tidy way of understanding how the sermon can be, in Austin's words, a performative act. All religions can be said to be like languages or cultures in that they enable us to operate within a certain worldview; they provide symbols and rules for putting those symbols together in meaningful ways. To be religious is to use those symbols in the prescribed ways; the symbols and the rules enable religious experience. For Christians, the primary source of such symbols is the Bible, and the theological rules that govern our use of these symbols is also derived from the scriptures. The average Christian imbibes the biblical symbols and theological rules while sitting in the pew. Thus the sermon takes on the crucial role of establishing the connection between the scriptural world and the everyday life of the congregation. The sermon in effect becomes a world of its own. It beckons the listener to live there.

News And Information

Of course, expressions like "cultural-linguistic" and "performative act" are scholarly technical terms, part of a culture and language far removed from the language of the pulpit. A simple, plain-English way of understanding what I am trying to get at here is provided by the novelist and essayist Walker Percy. In his essay "The Message in the Bottle,"[14] Percy imagines a castaway on an island, his memory lost in a shipwreck. The island is a pleasant place, the natives are friendly, the culture advanced, and the castaway makes himself at home. Yet each day the castaway is drawn to the beach where he first found himself, confused and remembering nothing of his previous life. There he regularly comes upon bottles washed up by the waves. The bottles, tightly corked, each contain a single sentence written on a small slip of paper. The messages are on diverse subjects, and the bottles soon pour in by the thousands, with messages like,

Lead melts at 330 degrees.
2 + 2 = 4.
Chicago, a city, is on Lake Michigan.
A war party is approaching from Bora Bora (a neighboring island).
There is fresh water in the next cove.

The castaway notes that there are two major types of messages, and the distinction between them lies not so much in the nature of the message, but in the state of the reader. Take the sentences "Lead melts at 330 degrees" and "There is fresh water in the next cove." Both sentences, if true, contain useful bits of knowledge, but the second will read differently to the thirsty castaway, let alone someone dying of thirst. Similarly, the knowledge that "2 + 2 = 4" is something every island schoolchild learns early in life and is not particularly remarkable, while the responsible islander who learns that "A war party is approaching from Bora Bora" is compelled by civic duty to convey that information to the authorities as soon as possible. Knowing where to find a place called Chicago takes on a different importance in turn for an airplane pilot, a mapmaker, or someone who learns that her sweetheart has just moved there.

Thus Percy makes the distinction between "knowledge" and "news," based on the situation of the receiver. Knowledge can be arrived at anywhere and everywhere, but news is relevant to the concrete predicament of the hearer of the news. The hearer can be objective about knowledge, but not about news. The significance of any information depends on the situation of the hearer; even the seemingly pure knowledge that "$E = mc^2$" can be news of the greatest significance to the scientist working desperately on a weapon to stop that approaching war party from Bora Bora. But the politicians who allocate funds for the scientist's military project must accept his word that such a weapon is feasible and await the outcome of his experiments with no guarantee that their money has been well spent. A piece of news, unlike pure knowledge, is not confirmable at the point of hearing. If someone appears on a sand dune and shouts, "Come with me, I know where there is water," the man dying of thirst does not pause to analyze the sentence — if the newsbearer appears to be a credible person, the thirsty man will follow. One who hears news will respond according to the predicament. Percy gives this example:

> *If a congress of scientists, philosophers, and artists is convening in an Aspen auditorium in order to take account of the recent "sentences" of their colleagues (hypotheses, theories, formulae, logics, geometries, poems,*

> *symphonies, etc.), and if during the meeting a fire should break out, and if then a man should mount the podium and utter the sentence "Come! I know the way out" — the conferees will be able to distinguish at once the difference between this sentence and all the other sentences which have been uttered from the podium.*[15]

If the newsbearer, though a stranger, appears sober and trustworthy, the conferees are likely to follow.

Percy goes on to make the distinction between "island news" and "news from across the sea." The news that "There is fresh water in the next cove" will be received gladly by our thirsty castaway, but it will never tell him who he really is, where he came from, and why he is there. No matter how involved he may be in the affairs of the island, there will always be a nagging feeling of alienation; the castaway always knows, at some level, that he belongs elsewhere. He is not really at home on the island, and no bits of island news will satisfy his soul. This sort of news, says Percy, cannot be placed in a bottle, for it requires a newsbearer — someone commissioned with the authority to carry the news, an apostle who is distinguished by the peculiar gravity of the message. An unsigned slip of paper in a bottle gives the castaway no way of evaluating the credentials of the one who wrote the message; it may contain purported news from the castaway's homeland across the sea, but the castaway has no way of knowing that it is not a hoax, perhaps a bit of disinformation sent from Bora Bora to confuse and divide the civilians. The castaway will require a sober, credible ambassador if he is to accept this news. He cannot determine the state of affairs across the sea by even the most minute examination of the island, or of the things that wash up on its shores; he is dependent on one who comes from across the sea to bring this news.

While Percy's concern was not the sermon *per se*, the preacher's application will be obvious: sermons will contain not just "knowledge" but "news," and news from across the sea at that. To modify one of Percy's illustrations, imagine a group of biblical scholars sitting in an auditorium with others of their guild as the members one by one walk up to the podium and utter sentences with which they may not all agree, that may or may not be true, sentences such as,

I was a woman.
The Hebrew incursion into Palestine was gradual and incremental rather than violent and sudden.
The historical Jesus was more like a Cynic philosopher than a rabbinic teacher.

Suppose, as they are listening to these sermons, that the fire alarms go off, and they begin to see smoke filtering in under the doors of the auditorium. And suppose that as all this is happening someone walks to the podium and in a calm and detached voice — just like every other voice heard from that podium on that day — announces, "I know the way out; please follow me." The biblical scholars will not treat this sentence like every other sentence uttered from that podium that day. They will not write this sentence in their notebooks, debate it in their minds, formulate statements to be delivered at the question and answer period, or decide to write papers about it. It will be for them "news," and even the most absent-minded of them will act on it immediately.

A sermon that merely repeats the utterances of biblical scholars stops short of being the good news of God's grace. Because the listeners, if we are to believe the Bible, are in a predicament — the smoke is already seeping through the cracks in the doors. The sermon both recognizes the predicament and shows the way out. The utterances of biblical scholars may provide useful information for the preacher hard at work discerning the biblical message for a particular Sunday, and the preacher may or may not repeat some of those sentences to the congregation. But the preacher's main focus is news, and news is transformative. The radical message of Christianity — that we do not owe our existence to ourselves, we cannot save ourselves, and we do not get what we deserve — changes our perception of reality. We are not of this world. The purpose of the sermon is to allow the hearers to see the smoke filtering in and to invite them to follow out the doors and into that new world. The sermon, above all, says "Come!"

Let me return to Percy's castaway, who by now may have found his way from the beach into the church. The sermon he hears from that pulpit must offer news, and not just island news. The sermon is not about becoming a better and more responsible islander, nor is it about how to improve island culture and reform corrupt island institutions. It certainly does not consist in telling the poor islanders what they are doing wrong. After all, the castaway does not come to church for mere information, no matter how true or good, and he gets his island news from Dan Rather and *Nightline*. Neither deep thoughts about the state of the island nor any amount of important island knowledge will speak to the soul of castaways, who are not really islanders after all, but owe their existence to One across the sea. The sermon is about who we really are as castaways, about how someone came from across that sea to tell us who we are and how we came to be in this predicament, and to bring us the means to live according to our true nature. This is welcome news, and to hear it is to see the island in a new light. The castaway who hears the apostle enters a new world.

That which is news — particularly news from across the sea — is transformative. It creates a new reality. To utter news is a performative act. Thus Percy, like Austin and Lindbeck, ultimately speaks of language as a system of words and grammar that enables one to experience reality. Language in general creates as much as it describes, and religious language creates in especially profound and significant ways. The sermon that conveys not just information but also news will effect a change in the world of the hearers. That sermon will absorb old worlds in the creation of a new one.

The Word, Living And Active

That the spoken word is creative and active is no stranger to Christian tradition. "Then God said, 'Let there be light'; and there was light" (Genesis 1:3). The Hebrew *dabar* could mean "event" as well as "word." In the New Testament, influenced by the Jewish Wisdom literature and nonbiblical Greek traditions, the Word (Greek *logos*) was personified: "The Word became flesh and lived among us" (John 1:14; cf. 1 John 1:1; Revelation 19:13). Jesus as God's Word is attributed the power of creation:

> *In the beginning was the Word, and the Word was with God, and the Word was God. He was in the beginning with God. All things came into being through him, and without him not one thing came into being (John 1:1-3; cf. 1 Corinthians 8:6; Colossians 1:15-17; Hebrews 1:2).*

Throughout biblical tradition, God's word is a creative force that makes something happen in the world and among the people called by God. "Indeed, the word of God is living and active, sharper than any two-edged sword, piercing until it divides soul from spirit, joints from marrow; it is able to judge the thoughts and intentions of the heart" (Hebrews 4:12).

Nor is the power of the spoken word a surprise to any working pastor. When the pastor walks into the hospital room and says, "I'm praying for you," the atmosphere in that room changes; the change is even greater when the pastor utters a prayer on the spot. The people in that room know that this is not "so much talk," because the words are deeply personal and meaningful. The most important words are hardest to say — which is why evangelism from bumper stickers and passing out tracts in shopping malls seems so gauche; the gospel cannot be reduced to a slogan, and the newsbearer seems less than credible when mouthing in the same breath both "God" and "Big Mac."

What the pastor learns in the hospital room (or for some, in the McDonald's and the shopping mall) applies equally to the pulpit. Real, serious preaching is difficult precisely because of the power of the spoken word. If your hand is not shaking before the sermon, if your mouth is not dry, perhaps it should be. The preacher stands before the congregation and mouths that most important word, "God," and then sits back to see what happens as the Word is set loose to do its work among the people. By its very nature, the pulpit is a position of immense power.

Some frustrated pastors may reply that they have been preaching for years and the congregation has shown absolutely no indication that they remember anything that has been said. But the power of the Word is not the power to induce perfect recall among the hearers. Rather, preaching provides the images, symbols, and thought forms by which a new imaginative world is created. While sometimes a particular sermon may produce an immediate reaction, generally the effect of preaching is felt in a congregation over a period of time, the sermons in effect providing the raw material by which a congregation builds its image of itself and the world in which it lives.

Knowing that preaching's legacy is cumulative suggests both a strategy and a danger. The strategy recognizes that the sermon works best as a symbol rather than a directive. The goal is to refresh the congregation's imagination and to repopulate its world with grace-filled figures. Amos will walk the streets of the city, and Mark will sit with them in the pew. Injunctions against, say, racism are well and good, but mere exhortations do not compete with the images of dark-skinned criminals gleaned from *Cops* and *Hard Copy*. To combat racism, the preacher must fill the sermon with positive images of Asians, Hispanics, and African-Americans; pictures can be replaced only with new pictures. If the sermon is the source of the symbols and images by which the congregation will form Christian consciousness, then the preacher will work to make those symbols and images vivid and alive in the sermon. Mere logic simply will not do.

The danger of the power of the Word is found precisely in its strength: over time, the congregation will take on the image of itself offered by the preacher. People often become what you tell them they are. Here is where the hortatory sermon proves the point. For example, one congregation listened to ten years of sermons that complained bitterly that the denomination was in decline, church attendance was falling steeply, the budget was in arrears, and the congregation was gossipy about members and unfriendly to newcomers. The continuing burden of the sermon was to tell them to shape up. The underlying message was clear even when the congregation was not being directly attacked; said one regular attender, "I felt like I was being chided even when I didn't know what for." After ten years the new pastor found a congregation that saw itself and its denomination in decline, attendance dropping, the budget in arrears, the members gossiping about one another and unfriendly to visitors — in short, a congregation that looked much like the one described in the sermon for ten years. Hortatory preaching does have its effect, but it is rarely the intended one.

The images that will change the congregation into the likeness of the church are primarily biblical images. The primary focus of the sermon is to bring the biblical Word to bear on modern life. The task is tricky, because the preacher must find the intersection of Word and life. The Word is a strange, foreign, ancient one, from a culture and time about which few in the congregation have any extensive knowledge. However, since it is the Word, it speaks on some level to every generation; the preacher must find that point of intersection. Pick too trivial or peripheral an entry point, and the profound nature of the message may be lost; the sermon, listeners will say, used the text as a pretext. Retreat into abstract obscurities, and the preacher will soon be awakened by the snores of the congregation. The most effective preaching places biblical images alongside appropriate pictures drawn from everyday life, and allows one to interpret the other.

Ultimately, however, no matter how hard we work, no matter how carefully crafted our sermons, what happens in the sermon is out of our control. The sermon is, like life itself, an event of God's grace. Christian tradition has consistently invoked the Holy Spirit as the source of the divine word, and the Spirit, John reminds us, blows where it will. To stand in the pulpit is to enact the message; the sensitive preacher will experience the truth that we are not our own, but owe our existence to an Other beyond and outside ourselves. Once the words leave the preacher's mouth, they cannot be taken back, nor does the preacher have any control over what use the congregation puts them to. The only sensible reaction could be that of Isaiah, to protest that even if a person of unclean lips could utter the proper words, the people of unclean ears would not be able to hear them. Truly we are right to be afraid; the burning coal brought to Isaiah's lips touches ours as well. One trusts that the Spirit brings a similar brand to the ears of the listeners. The Word of God is living and active, beyond our reach or power. The preacher simply by standing in the pulpit proclaims belief in the grace of God. To preach is to believe.

Conclusion

The sermon is sometimes (mis)understood as a speech that tells people to do something, a notion almost but not quite correct. It is not so much that the sermon provokes action, but that the sermon must act. The audience cannot be expected to perform unless the sermon goes to work first. The sermon must do something: what it must do is create a world, a world we call the Church.

That world, above all, will be a scriptural world. The sermon as an exposition of Christian scripture will paint a picture with the palette the Bible has provided. But this does not mean that the sermon will reduplicate that dusty exegetical paper written for NT 101, nor are we ready to open a commentary, or even an annotated Bible. No — before reading the Bible, or to be more accurate, while reading the Bible, the preacher must read the people. This complicated task of reading is the next stop on our road toward the Sunday sermon.

---

1. My source for this section is Brian Wren, *What Language Shall I Borrow? God-talk in Worship: A Male Response to Feminist Theology* (New York: Crossroad, 1989); quotations are found on pp. 50, 38, 49. Wren draws on Brian Easlea, *Fathering the Unthinkable: Masculinity, Scientists and the Nuclear Arms Race* (London: Pluto Press, 1983), p. 85.

2. Joseph Conrad, *Under Western Eyes,* cited in Michael McKenna, *The Stein and Day Dictionary of Definitive Quotations* (New York: Stein and Day, 1983), p. 204.

3. J. L. Austin, *How to Do Things with Words.* Ed. J. O. Urmson and Marina Sbisà. 2nd ed. (Cambridge: Harvard University Press, 1975). Austin's theories were extended in John R. Searle, *Speech Acts: An Essay in the Philosophy of Language* (Cambridge: Cambridge University Press, 1969).

4. Austin calls the first kind of performative utterance "illocutionary," and the second kind "perlocutionary." Since my argument does not depend on the

preacher learning these arcane technical terms, I will speak simply of the "first kind" and the "second kind" of performative utterances.

5. George A. Lindbeck, *The Nature of Doctrine: Religion and Theology in a Postliberal Age*, (Philadelphia: Westminster, 1984). For a brief, clear introduction to Lindbeck's thought, see Mark L. Horst, "Engendering the Community of Faith in an Age of Individualism: A Review of George Lindbeck, The Nature of Doctrine: Religion and Theology in a Postliberal Age," *Quarterly Review* 8 (Spring 1988), pp. 89-97.

6. Lindbeck, p. 32.

7. *Ibid.*, p. 33.

8. *Ibid.*, p. 62.

9. *Ibid.*, pp. 15-25.

10. *Ibid.*, p. 35. Emphasis his.

11. *Ibid.*, p. 118.

12. *Ibid.*, p. 117.

13. See Lindbeck, p. 132.

14. Walker Percy, "The Message in the Bottle," in *The Message in the Bottle: How Queer Man Is, How Queer Language Is, and What One Has to Do with the Other* (New York: Farrar, Straus and Giroux, 1975), pp. 119-149.

15. *Ibid.*, p. 138.

Chapter 2

Reading The Readers

In my homiletics classes, I regularly ask beginning students to picture themselves in the study Monday morning, ready to start work on Sunday's sermon — what do they do first? Usually they answer, "Read the texts [found in the lectionary for that Sunday]." To their intense discomfort, I then point out that this is not the starting point of their textbook, Fred Craddock's *Preaching*. Craddock's chapter on "Interpretation: The Listeners" comes before the chapter "Interpretation: The Text." "Giving disciplined time and attention to the interpretation of one's listeners is critical for preaching," says Craddock.[1] One begins by reading the listeners.

My students give the common-sense answer; every preacher knows that the first thing you're supposed to do is pick a text and read it. Craddock himself notes that one could just as easily begin with the text as with the listener, since text and listener are inextricably intertwined. But even when beginning with the text, one begins with the listener, since the two entangle on a deep, subconscious level fundamental to the very act of reading. The advantage of consciously beginning with the listeners is that the preacher benefits from a close look at the inner process. Reading a text always assumes a prior reading of the reader, and the better we understand this truth, the better readers (and preachers) we will become.

The careful reader of this text will note that I have already slipped from referring to the congregation as "listeners" to calling them "readers." This is not really a slip; my argument is that the congregation is itself composed of readers, who in certain ways read the text with the preacher, while reading a text composed by the preacher and called the sermon. I believe that even in the preacher's study, the congregation is reading over her shoulder. This process is complex and is carried out largely unknowingly by both parties. The preacher may view herself as a prophet bringing a divine Word unsullied by human opinion, while the congregation regularly not only misses the preacher's point but assumes that the point they heard was the intended one. Over time, with luck and persistence, a congregation may become better readers of their preacher and her sermons, just as the preacher will learn better how that congregation hears, and return to the study with this insight. Little of this interpretive activity takes place on a conscious level; it is part and parcel of our continuing participation in that social unit called a "congregation." As preachers, our audience — our congregation — influences us as readers in ways we are only dimly aware of. They compose part of the interpretive community in which we work. We preachers in turn supply the congregation with the tools which build that interpretive community.

Listening Readers

My use of the phrase "interpretive community" is indebted to a branch of literary criticism known as "reader response criticism." Reader response critics are a diverse lot rather than a coherent, single-minded school, but they all agree that the reader does a substantial amount of the work in the interpretation of a text. One reader-response critic, Wolfgang Iser, speaks of "gaps" in literary texts, empty spots which the reader must fill with the necessary literary, social, cultural, psychological, historical, or other kind of information in order to understand the text. Reading, for Iser and other reader-response critics, becomes a process of forming and revising expectations; as the reader moves along, new information is added, and gaps are filled and refilled.

> *Whenever the reader bridges the gaps, communication begins. The gaps function as a kind of pivot on which the whole text-reader relationship revolves. Hence the structured blanks of the text stimulate the process of ideation to be performed by the reader on terms set by the text.*[2]

Readers, according to Iser, try to bring coherence to a sometimes incoherent or partially-coherent text by taking the disparate parts and creating a coherent whole. Thus the text, to some degree, is actually created by the reader, who abstracts from the written page a sense of the meaning of the whole, forming opinions and revising them as necessary along the way. What is remarkable about the process of reading is not that texts contain gaps, but that readers are so persistent and competent at filling them in. Every reader treats every text to some extent as a mystery novel; one expects the text to have gaps, and one assumes it will provide sufficient clues for filling the gaps. While all this may sound like tedious labor, it is so deeply ingrained in our reading habits that we do not realize it is taking place; and besides, when we do notice the gaps and begin to think about how we might fill them in, we usually enjoy the process. Puzzling over gaps and ambiguities is part of what literary critic Robert Alter calls "the high fun of the act of communication."[3]

Here is an example of the kind of gap-filling that goes on with even the simplest texts. " 'What did you make of the new couple?' The Hanemas, Piet and Angela, were undressing."[4] The reader is only briefly if at all puzzled by the apparent lack of connection between the two sentences; one readily recognizes the literary convention here — the speech must be attributed to one of the two characters. A picture of the scene forms; the couple undressing is probably alone in a bedroom, if the usual customs are followed. The reader will assume that the two characters are human, not animals in the zoo (which do not wear clothes and thus would not need to undress). While the characters could be children, perhaps brother and sister, last name Hanema, the speech referring to the "new couple" would make more sense on the lips of married adults. That the actual reader of the original text has in hand a novel by John Updike titled *Couples* reinforces this supposition. But even the reader of the present book, reading the two sentences out of context, could determine as much. One could also surmise that the novel reader will learn more about Piet and Angela Hanema, and about the new couple, but that someone reading my book will learn no more about them unless they put down this book to take up Updike. There is no inherent or necessary reason, however, that the reader's conjectures about these first two sentences will be correct, but based on the reader's experience with undressing couples, novel-reading, and books about preaching, there is little reason to suspect otherwise. Only time, and continued reading, will tell for sure. The text provides no more than the raw materials; the reader must construct the meaning.

Another reader-response critic, Stanley Fish, has used this example.[5] Professor Fish once wrote an assignment on a classroom chalkboard; the assignment consisted of a list of names, all literary critics, centered on the chalkboard:

>Jacobs-Rosenbaum
>Levin
>Thorne
>Hayes
>Ohman (?)

Fish put the question mark after the last name because he couldn't remember how it was spelled. The assignment duly copied into notebooks and class being dismissed, a new class, which was studying seventeenth century religious poetry, filed into the room to see this same list of names on the chalkboard. Playful Professor Fish, hard at work on his reader response theories, told them it was the sort of religious poem they had been studying and asked them to interpret it. The students responded with a flood of gap-filling — the poem was shaped into the form of a cross or an altar, they said, and it contained mysterious allusions to Jacob's ladder, the virgin Mary (Rosenbaum, German for "rose tree," being a reference to Mary as the rose without thorns), Jesus' own crown of thorns, the tribe of Levi, and the unleavened bread of the Exodus. The final name, Ohman, was taken as "omen," "Oh Man," or "amen." Some enterprising student counted the letters and reported that the most prominent were S, O, and N. Even the question mark at the end was given significance as the mark of ambiguity between the Christian and Jewish referents of the so-called poem. Only the unfortunate Mr. Hayes proved resistant to this thoroughgoing attempt to read an assignment list as a religious poem.[6] On the whole, however, the list proved obliging to the students' interpretive skills.

Fish's point is not, as some would have it, that language is indeterminable and can mean anything you want, and thus means nothing. It is rather that what you see depends on what you look for. Students looking for an assignment list will see nothing more than a list of names. Students looking for poetry will see poetic qualities in the same list of names. They begin to look with poetry-seeing eyes; knowing that the conventions of poetry allow for densely-organized intricate webs of meaning, they unravel possible poetic meanings. In essence, they make a poem, because that is what they have been called on to do.

Note that both sets of students go through similar complicated acts of gap-filling. The students expecting an assignment list must determine that this is in fact what the professor is writing on the board, and if so, which authors are meant, and whether the references are to books or articles. On a more basic level, they fill other gaps that have long been an unconscious part of their being — they know what an assignment is, what to do with it, what a class is, when and where the class meets next, that the assignment must be done by the next class meeting, and so on. The acts of gap-filling here, however pedestrian, are no less complex than the interpretive process in which the poetry readers engage. Noting and performing an assignment, no less than interpreting a poem, is learned behavior.

Both groups operate as what Fish calls an "interpretive community." Both interpretations — that this list is an assignment, or that it is a poem — are the products of social and cultural patterns of thought. The assignment-takers have been trained by fifteen years of report cards hanging over their heads; the poetry-readers have learned (and similarly been rewarded for) complex acts of literary perception. There are no independent, freestanding readers who can look down on both groups and say, "Yes, you are right," or "No, you are wrong." All readers must work with a set of conventions, most of which operate on a subconscious level, some of which are occasionally brought to the foreground. The reading conventions are learned behaviors, imbibed over years of both explicit schooling and the other, less formal ways we all become accustomed to live in social groups such as families, schools, workplaces, towns, and nations.

To take another example, where the chemistry student sees the model of an atomic structure, an art student may see an interesting abstract statue, but a child may see only a toy made of colorful balls and rods that fit together like Lincoln Logs. The difference is neither in the model itself, nor in the personal idiosyncrasies of the onlookers. The chemist, the artist, and the child all have been trained within different frameworks — the chemist has spent long hours in the lab, the artist in the museum, and the child in the playroom. In short, they belong to different worlds. They each represent a different standard of interpretation held not in isolation, but in common with others in the lab, museum, or playroom. Each represents a different interpretive community.

Critics have often pointed out that reader response theories go against the common-sense view that language has one and only one meaning; if I tell you to take out the garbage, I do not want you to put out the cat, and you cannot shirk your garbage duty by claiming that my words could mean anything you desire. Fish would reply that the command seems plain precisely because we all belong to a community which understands that garbage must be placed on the curb or in the dumpster. The situation enables the utterance to have any sense at all; if I do not speak English, or have never handled a plastic garbage bag, the two syllables "garbage" are simply nonsense. Further, a reference to "garbage" differs in meaning depending on whether I am in the kitchen or the computer room. There is no "garbage" apart from our mutual understanding that we are speaking about this worthless material that must somehow be taken to the landfill. The plastic bag of kitchen refuse may exist in space and time, but until we agree on what it is, what to call it, and what to do with it, it is only a puzzle. We may not be conscious of this complex web of mutual understanding, because we have been watching people take out the garbage ever since we can remember and doing it ourselves for quite some time.

Language — the ability and means to communicate — is neither universal nor transcendent. Different interpretive communities can and do attach different meanings to the same set of utterances or circumstances, but language and cultural patterns are not indeterminate, they are determined by the community. This is a point which even reader-response critics themselves, not immune from cultural conditioning, sometimes fail to see. For example, both Iser and Fish tend to assume "coherency-building" as a feature of reading — that is, as a reader works through a text, the reader unconsciously tries to build the text into a coherent whole, no matter how disparate the parts. But coherency-building is actually a community feature, and different interpretive strategies place different values on coherence. One would not try to interpret an entire copy of *USA Today* as a coherent story; the easily-recognized newspaper convention is that many unconnected stories are reported simply because they are timely. In biblical studies, not all exegetes read for coherency; the source analyst is trying to find the seams in the text, while the feminist critic may argue that the text is ideologically inconsistent. The pursuit of coherence, like all other reading activities, is not a universal, but a learned behavior.

I like to think of Fish's "interpretive community" in the plural, because none of us live simply; we are members of several interpretive communities, not just one. The chemistry student may go from the lab to the museum, and no doubt once played with Lincoln Logs, or perhaps has a well-used old set at home in his child's playroom; one person can function in all three places. Every flesh-and-blood reader lives within a variety of communities, some of which overlap. To some extent, one is free to move about different communities without foreswearing citizenship in one or another, as our chemist may move from lab to museum to the playroom at home. Some interpretive communities, of course, will be mutually exclusive; spiritual allegories are not usually acceptable in seminary exegesis papers, but they may be the rule in the monastery or the cult. Some communities are voluntary; the chemist need not visit the museum, nor join seminary, monastery, or cult. Other interpretive communities are not so easily changed, and probably cannot be cast off, such as the community of English speakers, or those born in twentieth century America. Given the fragmentary nature of modern life, one may even live in several conflicting interpretive communities without even realizing it. A variety of social standards influence any interpretation.

Interpretive Communities And Congregations

I am obviously suggesting that a congregation is a certain kind of interpretive community, and a sermon, as a genre distinctive to that community, is governed by community rules. The rules are imbibed unconsciously as one sits and listens to sermons, though occasionally some (mainly the preachers themselves) receive formal training. Over years spent in the pew, one learns what is expected. For example, the pewsitter learns to sit quietly and listen, except in certain churches, and there to respond only in certain conventional ways; one may yell "Amen" in some places, but one does not raise one's hand and ask questions, as in school. The pewsitter expects the sermon to be a religious discourse of some sort, perhaps an exposition of a scriptural passage. Those who grow up listening to the same preacher may learn that a sermon always begins with a joke, always ends in "Thanks be to God, Amen," always contains a reference to a recent movie, or that it consists primarily of several stories strung together. A visiting preacher who omits the customary beginning and ending, never mentions a movie, and then casts the sermon into the form of an argument may be resented as an inferior interloper. Visiting other churches poses even more problems; our pewsitter is shocked to walk for the first time into a church where the custom is to have 45-minute sermons assisted by printed notes in the pew and fancy overlays on an overhead projector. When one changes preachers or churches, one must learn new rules and become part of a new interpretive community. These shifts, while they may involve some discomfort and thus be met with resistance, require no great adjustment for the average human adult being, who has been unconsciously switching between different communities (work, school, family) for some time.

It thus becomes apparent that one of the main jobs a preacher performs is establishing the rules for the interpretation of the sermon. While this may involve some formal coaching of the congregation, the bulk of this work is done simply by preaching. Over the course of many sermons, the congregation will learn what to expect and how to hear the preacher's sermons. They become socialized in her particular variety of sermon-making. Sure, they were resistant when she first came and started telling her stories; the former preacher, who had served for thirty years, never said anything that did not come straight out of Calvin's *Institutes*. But gradually a few people came around; she began to see more smiles when she looked out from the pulpit. As time went on, people would tell her that her sermons were getting better and better, though she had not varied her preaching style one iota. It is true that to some extent her preaching was now more on the mark, because she had gotten to know them better. The compliments, however, indicated mainly that they had gotten the knack of listening to her. Over time, the people had learned how to listen.

People hear not a sermon but sermons. Their listening habits have been formed over many years; those who have listened to many preachers, or one preacher who used a variety of styles, are more versatile in their ability to hear a particular sermon on a particular Sunday. A preacher cannot expect to change much (if anything) in their listening habits with a single sermon, but over months, seasons, and years a change will take place. The congregation will become an interpretive community, and their interpretive standards will to a large degree be set by the preacher.

The process I have described is idealistic and hampered by a few realities, not the least of which is that our congregations do not spend their entire waking hours sitting in the pew. They spend much less time listening to us than they do on the construction line, in the kitchen, mowing the lawn, or even watching a single weekly television drama. They thus belong to several different interpretive communities and are far more skilled at functioning in these communities than they are at listening to our sermons. All these communities share certain standards of communication, such as the use of English or another common tongue — otherwise, we could not move between them. Each different community, however, has slightly different ways of looking at things. The executive, for example, may speak in terms of being proactive in order to enhance production capacity, and his ultimate working concern is the bottom line. A lawyer speaks an entirely different language of torts and *habeas corpus* (language tortuously learned in law school), and her ultimate concern may too be money, unless she happens to be a legal aid lawyer on a small salary who sacrifices to see justice done. The scientist speaks yet another arduously learned language, but may be preoccupied with a successful experimental outcome, leaving the university administration to worry about budget. All these people may come home to the same development in the suburbs, be a part of the same PTA, and coach in the same soccer league — thus sharing after-hours communities though their working vocabularies would mystify each other. And of course, all come home to read the same newspapers and listen to the same radio stations. Each lives in several interpretive communities, some of which overlap.

And each may come to the same church to hear the same preacher on Sunday. It is perhaps amazing, considering the different vocations of congregational members, that the preacher can communicate at all. The sermon is directed to people who live in diverse worlds. Certainly they do not live where the preacher lives and works — they have not been to the hospital or nursing home this week, and if so it was to visit close friends or relatives, not perfect strangers, as is often the case for clergy. They have not struggled with a commentary by Raymond Brown, nor did they attend the clergy conference keynoted by the liberation theologian. They had no transients knocking on their back doors in search of a handout.

Fortunately, we all share some common ground as fellow English speakers, fellow citizens and community members, residents of a particular place and time. Those who come to church share a common set of behaviors and a common language that is usually spoken only in church or other religious settings. Church is a special interpretive situation. The working language of the Sunday service is not the language of the kitchen, the lab, or the law office. What is said there makes sense only there. The preacher's job is to help the people make better sense of it. Admittedly, one hopes that they will carry the fruits of their understanding to kitchen, lab, or office. But the language makes sense only and precisely because it comes out of the church — it is, as Percy puts it, news from across the sea, and not our native tongue. The miracle of the church is that it brings together people who live in such diverse worlds and makes them into one body; if this were not the work of the Holy Spirit, it would still qualify as a great mystery.

The implications for the preacher are enormous. The sermon as part of the liturgy is first of all a community-building tool. The members of the church may or may not be active in various groups — Sunday school, youth group, community outreach, altar guild — but they all sit through the same liturgy. They have a sense of being a like-minded community. They are formed as a people when they all sit in the same space and share in ritual words and actions. The atmosphere of prayer, hymns, readings, and fellowship sets the tone for what it means to be a part of this interpretive community. The sermon is the most explicit tool for the building of this community; here the worship leader has nearly complete discretion, no matter how ritualized the rest of the service. Preaching is neglected at the community's peril; ritual without interpretation soon becomes stale. Pastors frustrated with the congregation's sense of community and their ability to think and act as Christians may do well to take a hard look at the sermon: how does the sermon enable the formation of the community? What kind of interpretive community has the preacher been building?

Another implication is that the preacher herself will be moving in and out of different interpretive communities. The preacher has been trained, usually in a seminary, to operate in the peculiar world of theology and religious studies. After long training, one has learned to use words such as exegesis, pericope, redaction, and infralapsarianism. These words are part of the technical language of this sort of academic training, and like all technical language, we use it because it provides a shortcut; it is easier to say "infralapsarianism" among ourselves than to say "the less rigid Calvinist predestinarian theory which holds that God appointed human beings to salvation only after the Fall" every time we wish to refer to this idea (and even our definition of the term includes words that make sense only to those who understand words such as "Calvinist," "predestinarian," and "the Fall"). Using the shortcuts not only saves time, but it performs a community function: learning the language allows one to enter and become a part of the community. New seminarians cannot be incorporated into the seminary community until they learn how to use this language; when they learn how to use it well, they show that they have been educated. When the preacher graduates and moves into her first church, however, the tables have turned. Few if any in this church have been to seminary, and if they have heard words from the technical language of theology, they probably are not fluent in them. They may be more fluent in such theological language as may be a part of hymnody or liturgy, but even some of those words may be no more than familiar, comforting syllables: "I know someone once told me what that meant, but I always have to look it up." The graduating seminarian moves from one interpretive community to another, very different, one.

In my preaching classes, I have often heard students use the technical language of theological studies in their sermons. Afterwards, I have always told them not to, because congregations generally had neither been to seminary nor read the same books as seminarians, and so would not understand the language. Some students have become quite upset, insisting, "My congregation is highly educated, and we have excellent adult theological education." That may be so, I say, but the technical terms are still out. Educated congregations, while they may raise the standard of discourse, still do not share the technical vocabulary the pastor so arduously learned in seminary. On the contrary, they spent their school time working just as hard at learning the language of business, medicine, literature, or law. They have their own professional categories and are part of different interpretive communities. How would the pastor like to sit through a lecture on "the biogeographical study of marsupial carnivores, with special reference to borhyaenids"? No less will a congregation enjoy a sermon filled with Greek, Hebrew, or Latin words, along with references to "exegetical considerations" and "soteriology." Even more familiar words like "sin" may prove difficult, since "sin" in popular connotation has a meaning very different from its biblical and theological usage.

David Buttrick has argued that the language of the sermon consists of a limited vocabulary of ordinary words shared by most people, no matter how or where educated. Seminary graduates have a vocabulary of about 12,000 words. By contrast, the average member of our congregations uses about 7,500, including about 2,500 technical, vocational terms, from the secretary's "directory tree" to the plumber's "T-joint" to the farmer's "haycock" to the nurse's "pulsimeter." Subtract a few more expressions of purely local color, and there remains a shared common vocabulary of about 5,000 words — little more than the vocabulary of the Greek New Testament.[7] I don't know where Buttrick gets his figures (he doesn't say), but I imagine he is close to the mark. The purpose of the sermon is above all to communicate, and communication is best focused on a specific audience or interpretive community. If that interpretive community is composed of a general slice of humanity, as the normal church congregation is, then the language of the sermon must be the language shared by all. The preacher will do well to study the language of local and national newspapers and popular magazines such as *People*. Or one may close the eyes and listen to a good television announcer (pick radio and closing eyes becomes unnecessary). The popular media are designed to appeal to the common denominator, and while their content may be crass (so we usually say "the lowest common denominator"), the language is right on target, or they wouldn't stay in business.

Could not one use the sermon to teach congregations such theological shortcut-words as may be useful? No, probably not. Learning a new technical vocabulary is a difficult, laborious process. It is not uncommon to see seminarians at the end of a year of training misusing words they learned the first day, or misspelling "pericope" as "periscope." The preacher cannot hope to initiate the congregation in theological discourse by briefly alluding to theological terms in a once-a-week, fifteen-minute speech, with no audiovisual aids, not even a chalkboard (remember how long it took you to figure out the difference between "exegesis" and "hermeneutics"). Unlike a book, the hearer of a sermon has no chance to go back and reread until light dawns. The mere repetition of technical terms (and this goes for Greek and Hebrew words) is probably heard as gibberish. (It reminds me of the time a seminary buddy, who had been reading a section of Gerhard von Rad's *Old Testament Theology* that was liberally punctuated with unpointed, untranslated

Hebrew, came in and announced that "Von Rad thinks the most important concept in the Bible is 'squiggly-dot.' ")

And besides, the preacher who assumes theological literacy ignores what I call the "one stranger rule." When I first began to teach preaching, I asked beginning students to prepare their sermons with a real audience in mind: the rest of the class. I soon found myself hearing sermons which proclaimed, "We've left our homes to come to this strange place," and "Soon we'll leave this testing ground and go out to seek our true ministries" — in short, sermons that spoke eloquently to the situation of my students, but excluded me! The students quickly forgot that the "real audience" of the class included not just fellow students, but also a professor. Further, the students, knowing their colleagues well, aimed pointedly at those going through the seminary experience, punctuating the message with theological jargon and in-house jokes. So their sermons tended not to be suitable for the average congregation, where one cannot assume so narrow a perspective. I decided that while these sermons were truly appreciated by the students, they were not good practice for the wider, more diverse audiences these students would soon be facing. I began telling my classes to imagine as their audience the class itself, including both students and instructor, and one invisible, make-believe member in addition — a stranger who just came in off the street. After all, in almost any church on almost any Sunday, that could be the case — there could be a stranger, new to this church, perhaps new to any church, sitting in that back pew. These people, as far as the preacher knows, have no theological training whatsoever. The sermon must not exclude such as these. The "one stranger rule" is more than a training tool; it is good policy for any preacher in any congregation. The preacher who forgets the one stranger in the congregation (or the class) sounds, for lack of a better word, parochial — at a time when the message should be universal.

This does not mean that we cannot use the words of the Bible or speak of theological concepts. It simply means that we must do so in the language of the people. Jesus spoke in the language of the people, talking about such simple things as a lamp and a lost coin, and most of the gospel stories require no unusual vocabulary. Some of the most complex passages in the epistles of Paul or the letter to the Hebrews pose special problems, as the language and background are obscure to modern people, but even these can be successfully translated into a modern colloquial language if handled carefully. Theological concepts can be expressed in ordinary English, and once they are in English there is really no reason to introduce the theological term, unless one is planning to assign the congregation some Moltmann or Macquarrie as homework. Those members of the congregation who wish to engage in formal theological discourse can attend a class with all the appropriate learning aids, and will probably be delighted later to recognize a complicated theological concept presented so simply in a sermon; as for the rest of the congregation, they are looking for something they can easily take out of the church with them. As we shall see in a later chapter, it is a matter of putting the abstract into the concrete, and the unfamiliar into a familiar context.

If the language of theological studies is not useful in the pulpit, why use it at all? For that matter, why bother going to seminary to learn it in the first place? Simply because theological language is a shortcut, and it allows us to communicate with others in our guild, particularly the scholars and thinkers among us, who tend to use that language exclusively. Learning the shortcuts of theological discourse allows us to access the help provided by a host of commentators, essayists, theologians, and thinkers who provide basic research services. It also allows us to talk among ourselves more easily and precisely. Above all, it is necessary if we are to do our jobs as biblical and theological experts. Preachers are popularizers, and as such we must have something to popularize. Theological education provides needed depth and breadth to our preaching. As I shall argue in a later chapter, the language of exegesis, hermeneutics, and ecclesiology may not be found in the words we speak from the pulpit, but it is essential to the process that lies behind those words.

If any of this is hard to accept, it is due to the simple rule that cultures tend to be exclusive. Unless confronted with evidence to the contrary, members of a culture usually assume that their way of doing things is the only normal way, it is the "human" way (like the Indians in the Dustin Hoffman movie *Little Big Man* who called themselves not "Indians" but "human beings" — white folk, who did not act humanely, were not "human"). Both seminaries and parishes operate in the same exclusive fashion. What seemed normal ways of speaking, thinking, and acting will seem archaic (perhaps nostalgic) to the seminary graduate returning for the tenth-year reunion. The young graduate may not be able to conceive any way of communicating theologically other than standard theological discourse; the older pastor may have come to believe that seminary was a waste of time. Both fail to see that the preacher straddles two worlds, two interpretive communities. Theological weight without plain English communicates nothing, but if one steps away from one's training, the sermon degenerates into bumper stickers, self-help columns, and cute stories — fluff without content. The theologically-trained preacher works in a different world than the people in order to bring a message from the other side.

Congregations As Implied Readers

Once we have gotten used to the idea of a congregation as an interpretive community, we can begin to understand how the congregation plays a role in the preparation of our sermons, whether we know it or not. The sermon is prepared for a certain congregation, a certain interpretive community. The preacher brings to the biblical texts all sorts of knowledge and assumptions about that community and reads accordingly. Then the preacher prepares a sermon with that same community in mind. The congregation is implied from the beginning of the sermon process.

Again, literary criticism provides a helpful concept for understanding what is going on in the preparation of the sermon: the "implied reader." Literary critic Wayne Booth distinguishes between the real-life, flesh-and-blood reader of a particular text and the "implied reader" posited by that text.[8] As an author, I cannot anticipate who will pick up the text I am now writing, nor do I know when or where you, the flesh-and-blood reader, will read these words. No one who sets words down on a page can imagine where those words may end up. But to communicate, I must make certain assumptions about who you are and why you have picked up this book. For example, I assume you are not only interested in preaching, but are a preacher yourself, with some experience preaching and listening to sermons; at the least I assume you are learning to preach. I assume you are a parish minister or seminarian of a mainline denomination, relatively fluent in the language of theological discourse (as well as the English vernacular). I assume you are looking for help, a new way of thinking about and doing your weekly duty. I write within the cultural context of twentieth century America. I do not know how my words will sound in a hundred years, though I suspect they will be unbearably dated. In all these assumptions, and also further assumptions I may not be conscious of, I am positing an "implied reader." You, the flesh-and-blood reader, may be all of the above, or you may lack one or more of these features — you may, for example, be an international student, using English as a second language, struggling to understand the strange cultural allusions and my American English. But even if you fit all my assumptions, you as a human being are much more than simply a reader of my text; you presumably will read other books that posit other implied readers, and you certainly must do something besides read books. The implied reader is not a human being; it is a textual construct, an ideal reader posited by the text and the reading process. Ultimately, you, the flesh-and-blood reader, must take on the persona of the implied reader to understand this text fully. You must figure out what kind of implied reader my text assumes, then take on the characteristics of that reader. If you are successful, and I have done a good job, you may have that experience of being lost in a book, that feeling that a text communicates so strongly that I the author am speaking directly to you, engaging you directly inside your head. The implied reader is the audience I build into the text, and which you must reconstruct from the text, in order for us to communicate. Again, the miracle of the reading process is that so much of this activity is deeply ingrained into our reading habits and takes place unconsciously.

When I use the term "implied reader" about sermons, I do so with some trepidation, because I do not want you to make any assumptions about sermon manuscripts or delivery based on this term. When I speak of the sermon as a "text" and the congregation as "readers" I am speaking in broad, figurative terms. I do not mean that a sermon is a written composition; in fact I believe just the opposite: the sermon is primarily an oral composition and cannot be completely reduced to the written notations we may take into the pulpit to enable us to get through the sermon. When I am asked on Saturday if my sermon is done, I inevitably reply, "The sermon is not done until it is preached" (and even then it may not be finished working on the people). When people ask if they can see a copy of my sermon, I look at them with puzzlement; the best I can do is show them the written remnants of what was an oral experience limited in space and time. You cannot publish a sermon in a book; at best you can publish your sermon notes, but even if they are word for word what you said from the pulpit, they are not the sermon. The sermon is a spoken event, delivered to a certain congregation in a certain context; even if repeated, it will be in dozens of subtle ways different. In some forms of literary criticism, it is normal to speak of activities, events, and unwritten communications as "texts"; for example, a night at the bowling alley, or a magazine picture layout, are "texts" composed of symbolic codes or behavior which have meaning and can be interpreted. I am willing to speak of a sermon as a "text" in that sense: the sermon is an event in which certain verbal and nonverbal symbols are presented for interpretation — like a written text, the sermon is an act of communication. I do not by that imply anything about the delivery of the sermon, whether the preacher writes a complete manuscript and takes it into the pulpit, or memorizes it, or just writes notes, or uses neither notes nor manuscript — any of these variations can produce excellent results. When I speak of the congregation as "implied readers," I literally mean that they are "implied listeners."

These implied listeners are posited by the preacher from the beginning of sermon composition. The preacher assumes many things about the congregation, some of them unconsciously. The congregation is assumed to be of a certain denomination. The preacher as a member of the larger community will know certain things about these flesh-and-blood listeners, and those items will form part of the constructed listener assumed by the sermon: what the socio-economic makeup of the community is, along with the general education level, down to the most mundane things like what it is like to shop at the local grocery store. The preacher, like the congregation, is aware to a greater or lesser extent of the major cultural movements and news events of the day, and these too may form part of the assumptions governing the posited implied listeners. As a pastor to this congregation, the preacher knows some very intimate details about the comings and goings of the people. While these details, being confidential, will not find their way into the sermon (nor any future sermons at any future congregations, lest the pastor appear to be a blabbermouth), they will subconsciously contribute to the preacher's picture of the implied listener.

The preacher can intentionally refine this portrait of the implied listeners. Stock advice found in every homiletic textbook suggests working the congregation into the sermon preparation process by imagining, one by one, the faces in the pews week after week, before taking up the pen. This helpful exercise is ignored only at the preacher's peril, as no text can be targeted so carefully as the one aimed at real people. The danger with this exercise is that it may result in exclusionary, excessively parochial, or in-house speech, like the sermons my beginning students would preach to each other. The "one stranger rule" is a good corrective, as is the proposal of Fred Craddock that the preacher begin the sermon process by imagining the listeners not only as congregation but as audience — not just as well-known friends and neighbors, but as strangers, a general slice of humanity.[9]

It is important for the preacher to understand that no matter how carefully constructed, the implied readers of the sermonic text are creations of that text, not real people. The preacher is, as the term says, implying something about the listeners. Real people are much more slippery and hard to get hold of than the personas assumed and projected by the preacher's imagination. Not even the wisest among us can predict all the variables of human behavior. The best we can do, especially in the few minutes allotted us, is make a few educated guesses and hope that we hit the mark. That we are sometimes greeted at the door with a radically strange interpretation of what we just said is but one indication that our grasp of our fellow human beings is tenuous at best.

It is precisely the slippery nature of the human beast that makes the concept of the implied listener such a valuable tool for the preacher. To some extent human beings are malleable; because they are free creatures, they have the ability to change. They sometimes take on whatever persona is offered them; indeed, they must, at least temporarily, if they are to understand what is being said to them. For example, if I have a complaint with a store manager, I may approach him in the manner of the customer who is always right. If the store does not follow that policy, the manager and I will have a hard time communicating, but if the usual rule prevails, the manager will take on the corresponding role of the helpful retailer, we will understand each other, and I will get my way. That brief moment of communication may carry over into my next encounter; I may be more assertive with everyone I meet all day. Of course, if I carry this role home with me, I am in danger of taking it too far and will quickly be set straight by my family. So too, the congregation must take on the offered role of implied listener if they are to get something out of the sermon. They must, at least for a short time, become what you tell them they are.

The role offered to the listeners must be both feasible and attractive. Many complaints about sermons can be traced to flaws in construing the audience — the preacher posited inappropriate implied listeners. Certainly sermons that use unfamiliar technical theological terms fall into this category; the congregation cannot take on the offered persona because they lack the knowledge, and the sermon is said to be "dull" or "boring." More pernicious is the feasible but unattractive implied listener. Suppose the preacher says, "It's a shame that people don't care enough to fill the pews to the brim every Sunday morning." The implied listener is invited to look down on the generic "people," who are uncaring non-attenders. The flesh-and-blood listeners, looking around at the empty pews, though they know that they too are "people," refuse to take on that unattractive persona, since they, after all, are here. Of the two personas offered, neither is pleasant, but the role of implied listener, who is superior by virtue of church attendance, is more attractive than the role of uncaring "people." A series of such statements will breed a haughty bunch who can't understand why more "people" don't join them every Sunday — though any visitor could tell them why in two sentences. The congregation becomes what was implied about them, resulting in a reality that contributes to the original problem.

The preacher who deals with a "problem congregation" may want to review sermon notes with an eye to the implied listeners. If there is a stewardship problem here, has the congregation often been told, even implicitly, that they are stingy? Replace lines that refer to tightly-wound purse strings with the acknowledgment that everyone wants to pitch in, and see the difference it makes. Is conflict rampant but kept under the lid, only to spill out at inappropriate and trivial moments? Fill your sermons with attractive people who deal with conflict openly and successfully, and you will invite your listeners to go and do likewise. Preachers who fuss at their congregation about apathy, gossip, and inattention are merely fueling the flames; they would do better simply to assume the best about them. The question is not only what kind of implied listener you have, but what kind of implied listener you want. I am not being Pollyanna here — the sermon will certainly pinpoint sin in all its forms and diagnose the ills of humanity. But the sermon cannot stop there. It must go on to preach the gospel, and the implied listener of that gospel is one who is not mired in sin, but liberated by God.

Recognizing the role of the implied reader of the sermon is an important tool for the proclamation of the gospel. Congregations can become what the preacher implies about them, for good or ill. Isn't it better to build them into our sermons as we would like them to be, and as we know they can be with God's grace, than to imply that they and God are not up to it?

Establishing An Interpretive Community

Our congregations are also fellow Bible readers with us. As part of our interpretive community, they join us every time we sit down with a text. When we read, we read with them in mind — we cannot hope but think ahead to implied readers of our own, those who will listen to our Sunday sermon. We bring the congregation to the text twice: once implicitly when we first engage the text, and again explicitly when we deliver the sermon. The congregation is there not just at the end but also at the beginning.

As interpreters working within certain boundaries, we cannot help but aim our interpretation in a certain direction. This holds for even the simple distinction between studying a biblical text to prepare for a Sunday school class and studying that same text in preparation for a sermon. The teacher comes at the text with a completely different approach because the audience is different. The teacher knows that the class is voluntary and self-selecting, that it studies (or does not study) at home, that it will benefit from audiovisual aids. The teacher is free to use charts and drawings, to divide the class into smaller groups, to use any teaching method that might cross the mind. All of this is known before the interpreter goes to work and hangs over the whole process of interpretation like a sign: "Enter Here." The situation and audience determine the interpreter's focus and the amount of depth and detail the interpretation will uncover. The teacher goes to the text looking for something to teach. The preacher, by contrast, cannot assume the same audience, nor will the preacher normally divide the congregation into small groups or use audiovisuals. The message stands or falls solely on the words the preacher utters. The preacher goes to the text looking for something to preach, knowing that preaching is not the same as teaching. Again, this may go against the grain of the received tradition which holds that there is a correct method for studying a text, resulting in a correct interpretation. It is true that the same interpretive methods are useful in both cases. Still, it is clear that texts can be put to many different valid uses, and thus have many different valid meanings. To bring one to understand a text is different from bringing one to hear the gospel in that text.

As an implied audience, the congregation interprets the text with us, though they may not be physically present in the room. We come to the text knowing who they are and how they look at things. We have done our preparatory exercises, visualized their faces, remembered their histories and their pains, thought of them as generic as well as specific human beings — as Bobby Jones who broke the stained-glass window with a baseball as well as a twelve-year-old adolescent, as Mr. Smith who loves to golf as well as a gray-haired widower. We have read the same newspapers they have read, watched the same television shows, shopped at the same stores. We know the ways this professional-class congregation differs from the working-class parish we served last. We have some idea of how they will see the biblical text that lies open before us. And we know how difficult it is to walk into a room full of strangers and preach the Word of God, so we are glad to have these familiar characters along with us at our desks beforehand.

There is no rule, however, that says that the congregation as interpreters must be present only in the mind of the preacher while the sermon is in preparation. While the implied readers are only a construct of the text, and as such must be imaginary, the preacher can certainly enlist flesh-and-blood readers from the congregation in weekly sermon preparation. Daily conversation offers an opportunity, if one will take the chance to say, "What do you think it means that the Kingdom of God is like a mustard seed?" or "What do you think of when you think of Noah's Ark?" There is nothing to stop a preacher from calling a trusted member of the congregation before Sunday and saying, "Let me run this idea by you...."

I would like to propose a more formal implementation of the idea that the congregation is an interpretive community out of which and for which the preacher works. Suppose the preacher picked a few parishioners and asked them to join in a covenant: this group will meet each week for so many weeks to study biblical texts to help the preacher prepare the sermon. Note that this is not a sermon review group, though review may take place; the purpose of this group is to receive tangible benefit from the congregation's role as an interpretive community. The format could be left to the group to decide, and the leadership could be lay, clergy, or rotating, but there would be no lectures; the goal would be to encourage the preacher and the people to interpret together. The primary goal would be understanding leading to proclamation, not devotional (the meditative African Bible Study method, for example, would not be helpful). If new people rotate into the group every six months or so, before long the preacher would have not only new insight into both text and congregation, but the pews filled with better, more attentive, and more sophisticated listeners.

Conclusion

I have argued that preachers are part of interpretive communities who produce texts called sermons containing implied readers that must be teased out by real, flesh-and-blood human beings, also members of various interpretive communities. The congregation reads the sermon by taking on the characteristics of the implied readers; the people interpret the sermon by listening and becoming the listeners the text proposes. The role of implied listener is posited by the sermon and must be both possible and appropriate. The task of the preacher is complicated by the existence of many different, overlapping interpretive communities. The preacher must find common ground and place there material brought over from the preacher's own distinctive community, the world of theological studies. What is harvested in one place must be planted in very different soil. Fortunately, the preacher has the congregation itself as a resource for both interpretation and transplantation.

The sermon grows out of and in turn builds up an interpretive community, the church. Preaching is a performative act. It creates a new world. The question remains what kind of world the preacher is seeking to build. The answer, as I have already stated, is a world shot through with the biblical witness. We now turn from reading the readers to reading the text.

---

1. Fred B. Craddock, *Preaching* (Nashville: Abingdon Press, 1985), p. 98.

2. Wolfgang Iser, *The Act of Reading: A Theory of Aesthetic Response* (Baltimore: Johns Hopkins University Press, 1978), p. 169.

3. Robert Alter, *The Pleasures of Reading in an Ideological Age* (New York: Simon and Schuster, Inc., 1989), p. 30.

4. My example is based on Terry Eagleton, *Literary Theory: An Introduction* (Minneapolis: University of Minnesota Press, 1983), pp. 74-77.

5. Stanley Fish, "How to Recognize a Poem When You See One," in *Is There a Text in this Class? The Authority of Interpretive Communities* (Cambridge: Harvard University Press, 1980), pp. 323-337.

6. Though one friend has insisted to me that "Hayes" is obviously a typo for "Hades," a thought that apparently did not occur to Professor Fish's class.

7. David Buttrick, *Homiletic: Moves and Structures* (Philadelphia: Fortress Press, 1987), pp. 187-189.

8. Wayne C. Booth, *The Rhetoric of Fiction*, 2nd ed. (Chicago: University of Chicago Press, 1983), pp. 420-435.

9. Craddock, *Preaching*, pp. 86-90.

Chapter 3
Reading The Text

A friend tells of walking into church on Mother's Day and reading in the bulletin the text for the day: "Out of the window she peered, the mother of Sisera gazed through the lattice" (Judges 5:28). The sermon title: "The Windows of Motherhood." The preacher praised the virtues of mothers, who look patiently at the children they love through the "windows" of care, patience, and hope. In keeping with the sentiment of the day, the preacher never bothered to mention that Sisera, the Canaanite general, was by this point in the biblical story long dead, having had a tent peg driven into his head by the plucky Jael (Judges 4:1-24).

I used to think that in the sermon, "Boredom is the root of all evil," to quote Kierkegaard.[1] But I have come to believe lack of depth is an even greater problem. If the boring sermon shows signs of being ill, the trivial sermon lies in the coffin. Too many sermons offer too little of substance. They pick up a theme and go on their merry way, barely skimming the surface of their supposed biblical foundation. "Never use the text as a pretext," an old preacher friend used to say, knowing how many sermons seem to do just that.

True, "The Windows of Motherhood" is an extreme example, a pretext that would be silly were not its subtext so gruesome. It does, however, represent a common study-to-pulpit transaction. A word or phrase is taken from scripture because of its resonances with a liturgical or pastoral situation, or with a trend in current affairs, or with one of the preacher's pet projects. This word or phrase becomes the catchword of the sermon, and a supporting structure of images, stories, and arguments is built up around it. Once the preacher has taken the catchword from the biblical text, there is no reason to refer to that text. There is certainly no reason to look at any commentaries (they might take the sermon away!) or other study aids, except to borrow a few good stories. The sermon deals with the biblical passage tangentially if at all; the text provides no more than a word for further meditation. It does not contribute any substantial meaning to the sermon as a whole.

Thus the story of the walking on the water in Mark (Mark 6:45-52) takes sermonic form as an exhortation to personal piety: Jesus went up on the mountain to pray (v. 46), but the disciples did not do their own devotions, and so they could not recognize him on the chaotic waters. The sermon describes the personal and societal chaos we face today and exhorts us to pray, so that we may know the One who walks toward us. The synagogue sermon at Nazareth (Luke 4:16-20) yields a sermon that asks, "Are your eyes fixed on Jesus?" despite the fact that those who fixed their eyes on him (v. 20) subsequently tried to throw him off a cliff (v. 29). And the parable of the Rich Man and Lazarus (Luke 16:19-31) provides fodder for a sermon on homelessness, using poor old Lazarus among the dogs as a starting place. The substance of the biblical text lies untouched in these sermons. One may suppose there are meat and vegetables here somewhere, but the preacher seems to be serving up potato chips and cheese balls.

The discouraged seminary professor may lament this as a sign that little or nothing was heard in class. The tired parish preacher looking back on such classes may counter that the lack was not in student attentiveness, but elsewhere — possibly the lack of a curriculum at all relevant to the task of preaching week in and week out. Again, academic expectations conflict with realities. The preacher has been trained to do good exegesis and perhaps did so for a while. She soon found that the rewards in parish life differed from those in the academy. The lively, bright, vivid chat with the congregation was given positive reinforcement; the oral equivalent of a heavy tome was greeted with stony stares.

Meanwhile, we preachers complain that the congregation is biblically illiterate. Of course they are — what have we done to encourage them to become literate? In the play *Mass Appeal*, Deacon Dolson reflects on his childhood memories of the Sunday sermon: "I thought Snoopy was one of the twelve apostles." Our sermons have taught them by example: the contemporary story, the joke, the modern example is everything. The Bible is not particularly important, except perhaps as a mantra. We have formed an interpretive community that expects the Bible to be handed out as abstract tidbits. Sentences that begin with "What Jesus meant to say was ..." tend to, as Craddock puts it, boil off the water and preach the stain in the bottom of the cup.[2] If not reduced to a single platitude, the biblical stuff must at least be sugar-coated and gotten through as quickly as possible. The preacher knows they are waiting to hear that funny story about Uncle Al.

Some preachers, uncomfortable with this state of affairs, are tempted to throw away both funny stories and seminary textbooks, and preach straight Bible. Tired of positive thinking, sociological analysis, and therapeutic messages, they seek a sermon of substance and thus revert to pre-critical exegesis of a quasi-fundamentalist sort. Form and redaction criticism do not preach, they have found, but the images, stories, and arguments of the Bible still have their inherent raw power. Some guilt feelings may remain ("I know there are two sources in this passage, shouldn't I tell them?"), but most academic questions, concerns, and conclusions can be bracketed as far as the congregation is concerned. If it won't make it into the sermon, why bother with it?

There is a better way. We need not swing between the shallow end of Sermon Lite and the murky depths of intellectual sacrifice. Recovering the Bible for preaching requires a new way of thinking about the Bible. If we don't know what to do with the Bible in the pulpit, it is perhaps because we don't know what to do with the Bible, period. We are unsure how the Bible fits into the life of faith and the proclamation of the gospel. The rules under which we were trained and our experience in the pulpit have not taught us all we need to know. Neither major alternative — neither the sterile analysis of academic training nor the uncritical readings of pop theologians — is particularly satisfying. We must strike out anew. It is time for preachers to rethink the rules of their interpretive community.

Reading Presuppositions

A heated debate over biblical authority continues to rage in the churches. The differences between the various parties can easily be demonstrated by visiting four churches in the same town on successive Sundays (let us grant, for the moment, that all these preachers are conscientious, and none will offer "The Windows of Motherhood"). The sermons will be diverse. In the first church, where the sign out front says "Conservative Evangelical," the sermon is a 45-minute study of one verse in Romans. The congregation, following in well-thumbed Bibles brought from home, takes notes. On the second Sunday, the sermon at the Roman Catholic parish treats issues of human rights in Bosnia. The congregation meets afterward to plan a congressional letter campaign. The third Sunday, a suburban Protestant church offers an analysis of the human need for fellowship and proclaims that the church is the family of God. The emphasis is not surprising, for the pews are noisy with children. On the final Sunday, the sermon at the staid old downtown Protestant church is simply one long story, no explanation. The congregation is in tears by the end, but goes out smiling.

Ask for an explanation, and you will hear four different appeals to scripture. The conservative evangelical preacher claims the primacy of the Bible and celebrates the many Bibles carried into the pews. Even one verse is the Word of God and so contains riches innumerable. The Roman Catholic priest, a liberation theologian, will disavow this kind of "proof-texting"; it is plain to him that the broad sweep of biblical tradition speaks eloquently about God's preferential option for the poor. The third preacher claims to offer the biblical answer to perennial human needs; "answer" is to be taken in general terms, as "proof-texts" will not find favor here either. The narrative preacher at the fourth church will, true to form, answer in parables: "You don't build a house and leave the tools lying around." Biblical literacy, or even interest in the Bible, is not assumed. When pressed, this last preacher may echo Harry Emerson Fosdick's barb that "only the preacher proceeds still upon the idea that folk come to church desperately anxious to discover what happened to the Jebusites."[3]

All the preachers agree on one thing and in their charitable moments may even grant their accord with one another. They agree that the Bible is important. In all cases, the preachers confess the authority of the Bible. Even the preachers who make little or no reference to biblical texts in their sermons will still claim to be standing under God's Word. Clearly, the issue is how the Bible is important, and thus how it is to be used from the pulpit. The differences in their preaching are due in large part to their different understandings of what biblical authority means. For the preacher to be clear about what a sermon is, the preacher must clarify how the Bible is authoritative.

Three Presuppositions: Religion Thinks, Feels, Or Does

I contend that the debate over biblical authority, and thus about the role of the Bible in the sermon, stems from different presuppositions about what theological statements are. I have found it helpful to view the various possibilities in light of the work of theologian George Lindbeck, whom we met in the first chapter of this book. Lindbeck, you may recall, suggests that there are three basic ways to view a theological statement. The first he calls propositionalist, the second experiential-expressivism, and the third, his own position, he calls the "cultural-linguistic" view. We might characterize the different positions as "Religion Thinks," "Religion Feels," and "Religion Does."

The first position, what Lindbeck calls "propositionalism" and what I have referred to as "Religion Thinks," is the common-sense notion that theological statements are simply propositions about reality. In answer to what religion is, the propositionalist tells you what he thinks; he makes statements about religious doctrines. Religion is seen primarily through cognitive assertions about the divine. In this view, to speak theologically is simply to make statements about reality; theological statements, like scientific or mathematical statements, can be either true or false. Understanding a theological proposition leads to faith and is itself faith.

The second way of theological thinking Lindbeck calls "experiential-expressivism." I have dubbed it "Religion Feels." In answer to what religion is, the experiential-expressivist tells you how he feels; he relates a feeling or experience associated with the divine. Religion is seen primarily through religious experience. Experiential-expressivism, according to Lindbeck, has been dominant in modern theological thinking since Schleiermacher. For most preachers, it is the presupposition underlying our seminary training. The experiential-expressivist sees theology as the expression of religious feelings, like Schleiermacher's "feeling of absolute dependence." One first has a religious experience and then seeks to explain it. Understanding follows faith.

The third position is Lindbeck's own "cultural-linguistic" model, what I have called "Religion Does." Ask a cultural-linguist what religion is, and he will describe how religion works. Religion is seen primarily through its functions. Religious faith is likened to a language or a culture consisting of a vast web of symbols and rituals that all have meaning, conscious and unconscious, for those who share them. In Lindbeck's view, religious language creates religious experience, not so much as statements about a reality outside ourselves, but as the basic ground rules under which we live our religious lives. Where the propositionalist utters true statements, and the experiential-expressivist tries to put words on ineffable experience, the cultural-linguist speaks in order to create.[4]

We may illustrate the difference between these three ways of thinking through a simple example: the biblical language about "demons." Propositionalism, the "Religion Thinks" position, asserts the reality of demons. The Bible simply makes true propositions, and nasty spiritual creatures called demons exist. There are no two ways about it, either real-life demons exist, or they are imaginary and thus meaningless; only statements that correspond to tangible reality have meaning. Propositionalists have no problem believing in widespread satanic cults, and they are not hesitant to participate in exorcisms, because demons are real creatures that interact on some level with human beings.

Experiential-expressivists, being "Religion Feels" people, see no scientific evidence for the existence of these invisible creatures and thus usually don't believe in literal demons. Nevertheless, they grant the experience of demons; that is, they allow that bad things happen to good people for no apparent reason and that pre-scientific people may attribute these misfortunes to the work of supposed demons. Experiential-expressivism may, however, see an analogy to similar bewildering forces at work in modern life. The experiential-expressivist preacher translates between ancient and modern experience, calling systemic, institutional evil "demonic";

the ancient and modern experiences of mysterious evil are seen as essentially the same.

Like the experiential-expressivist, the cultural-linguist, who believes that "Religion Does," may have doubts about the actual existence of demonic creatures, and may also see the analogy with modern systemic evil, but unlike the experiential-expressivist, the cultural-linguist sees the ancient and modern experiences as fundamentally different. Ancient people believed in literal, not figurative, demons; most modern Americans do not. But the cultural-linguist may use the image of the demonic as a way of understanding life. The demon becomes a symbol by which we understand that there are evil, uncontrollable powers, and that they transcend the individual bad acts of human beings. The ancient category of "demons" proves to be a useful image for seeing life as it really is. It jars our modern sensibilities enough to goad us into thinking and talking about an underside of society we would prefer to ignore.

Thus the three different approaches take very different views of the biblical language about the demonic. The propositionalist will insist on using the word "demon" because demons really exist. The experiential-expressivist will be terribly uncomfortable with this language and will try to translate "demon" into something else, using the word only figuratively. The cultural-linguist will use the language as a way of understanding reality, but will hold it lightly.

What is true about one biblical concept proves to be true about biblical literature as a whole. These three views about what it means to make a theological statement manifest themselves in differing attitudes about the Bible. Each has its own strengths and weaknesses, and each will approach the task of preaching the Bible in its own way.

The Bible And "Religion Thinks"

If one is expecting propositions, one will look for propositions in the Bible and may see the whole Bible as a series of propositions about and/or by God. "Religion Thinks" easily becomes "The Bible Thinks." This position feels natural to many people, and not just self-avowed fundamentalists. It reflects the prevailing prejudices of our time. Modern empiricism has colluded with common-sense realism to give preference to the statement of fact over the poetic metaphor. People usually value the empirical over the flight of fancy; it is hard for most Americans to imagine how something can be true without corresponding to some tangible reality. This is the argument of agnosticism in a nutshell: if God can be neither seen nor touched nor empirically demonstrated, can it be rational to believe in such a God? Statements about God or anything else are either true or false, and one must have proof.

Protestant fundamentalists seek such proof in a Bible that consists of trustworthy propositions by God. They rely on a simple argument: The Bible is God's Word. God cannot lie. Therefore the Bible contains no errors. If the premises are true, they argue, the conclusion must follow. Proceeding from the assumption that all theological truth is propositional, and that the Bible contains a series of propositions, the fundamentalist position is unassailable. It is logically consistent, and that is its appeal and its strength. If you grant the presuppositions, it is hard to deny the conclusions.

The problem with this kind of propositionalism is not with its logic but with its facts. The doctrine of biblical inerrancy is vulnerable to a thousand tiny details. As 200 years of biblical scholarship has shown with excruciating, meticulous care, biblical texts can be inconsistent in matters of fact, they are sometimes clearly wrong about history, and their viewpoints are often mutually exclusive. Commitment to biblical inerrancy is an assumption brought to the text, not the result of a thorough study of the text. The critical study of the Bible has been seen by fundamentalists as an attack directed at them, and in some sense it is — as criticism brings biblical inerrancy into question, it shakes the whole foundation. This accounts for the hostility of fundamentalists toward biblical critics, and for their intense efforts to disprove or discredit critical biblical study. The inerrantist finds each and every "alleged contradiction" an assault on the faith itself, since even one will bring the whole house crashing down. There is a whole cottage industry of publishing houses, books, magazines, and speakers devoted to solving this interpretive problem.

The assumption of inerrancy thus spawns an interpretive method: the Bible must be shown to be inerrant. What happens in fundamentalist exegesis is not that the Bible is shown to be inerrant, but that the Bible is consistently read as if it were inerrant. Propositionalists must engage in some quite complex and clever interpretive moves in order to play as fair as possible with both their beliefs and the text, but one too often has the feeling that the text is the loser. Thus divergent passages that speak of the same events must be harmonized at any cost; the historical Peter, the inerrantist may say, really denied Jesus six times that final night in the courtyard; we must allow for all those cock crows (two in Mark [14:30, 72], one in the others).[5] Unfortunately, all the gospels number the denials at a mere three (Matthew 26:34; Luke 22:34; John 13:38). Passages not easily harmonized must be said to refer to different events entirely; Jesus, for example, must have met two blind men in Jericho, one on the way in (Luke 18:35-43), and one on the way out (Mark 10:46-52), and had virtually the same exchange with both. Matthew, of course, speaks of two blind men and places them at the exit to Jericho (Matthew 20:29-34), but this could have taken place down the road from the lone blind man mentioned in Mark or maybe on another visit entirely. The unwieldy hermeneutical behemoths that sometimes result may astound outsiders as incredible lumbering beasts, but these seeming improbabilities are the source of satisfaction and joy for the interpreters themselves, who are working with complete precision and consistency within the system. Propositionalism of this sort results in a certain strategy of reading: the Bible must be read so as to be inerrant.[6]

Despite the labors of Protestant fundamentalists, or any brand of propositionalism (and propostionalism is certainly not limited to fundamentalism as commonly perceived), the Bible cannot be reduced to a series of propositions. It does not all fit into the genre of systematic theological treatise. The Bible is filled with narratives, parables, letters, poems, songs, proverbs, genealogies, and other literary forms. Not all of these forms lend themselves to propositionalism; for example, what, exactly, is being proposed when the Kingdom of God is likened to a few measures of leaven? The Bible, while it contains propositions, is not limited to them. It is more than one large proposition.

The Bible And "Religion Feels"

The crisis in biblical studies of the nineteenth century was a crisis of propositionalism. The cumulative weight of historical-critical biblical scholarship made it impossible to hold a doctrine of biblical inerrancy without severe qualifications. For many that doctrine died the famous death of a thousand qualifications. Biblical scholars could no longer honestly read these texts as flat propositions from God. Clearly, they were multi-layered, multi-sourced documents that had grown and developed through many generations of undeniably human activity. The Bible itself found propositionalism an ill-fitting garment. To accept the critical view of the Bible meant in the long run to abandon propositionalism. The fundamentalists were quite right to attack historical criticism; it undermined their very foundation. (That the issues are little changed is clear from the arguments of present-day defenders of biblical inerrancy, which differ little from those advanced by their forebears a century ago.)

The onslaught of nineteenth century biblical criticism led theologians to consider how a God who cannot be proved can be intellectually respectable. The theological model in which nineteenth century biblical critics took refuge was, in Lindbeck's terms, experiential-expressive, the "Religion Feels" model. God could not be proved, but people clearly had religious experiences all the time. Perhaps the "truth" about religion was to be found not in abstraction but in concrete human experience. The truth about God was to be found in the undeniable truth that people are religious or become religious, sometimes in dramatic ways. One who has a mystical experience cannot prove that he has met God; nevertheless, the mystic is himself convinced and has so ordered his life.

With the widespread acceptance of historical criticism, the Bible could not be seen as a series of propositions about and/or by God. It could, however, be taken as a representation of various experiences of God. Inerrancy was rendered irrelevant; feelings, not propositions, were the important truths. The Torah did not have to be the composition of Moses, as long as it expressed significant truths about the religious sentiments of the Hebrew people. The Gospels need not reflect a historical Jesus, but only a Christ of faith. In fact, biblical stories need not have any factual underpinnings, as long as they had a basis in legitimate religious impulse; Jesus need not have risen on the third day, if one can rely on Peter's intuition of his continued presence.

An experiential-expressivist model solves the problems of propositionalism only to create new ones. For one thing, experiential-expressivism assumes what it cannot prove, that all religious experiences are basically the same. It imposes a unity that is not there; the religious experience of Moses and that of Peter are radically different — it is one thing to proclaim that God is liberator of the people and quite another to proclaim that human liberation is accomplished through the resurrection of a certain human being. It is not that different words refer to the same experiences. Different words virtually guarantee different experiences. Experiential-expressivism on this count proved more durable for Christian theology than for the study of comparative religion. The religion of Moses and that of Paul at least fall within the same religious tradition and so have some genetic similarities; the conceptual divergence between the religion of Moses and that of a Buddhist monk is a yawning chasm.

Another problem with experiential-expressivism is that it merely presses the problems of propositionalism back a level. The Bible becomes a source book of religious experience. The biblical theologian must uncover the experience that lies behind the text. Instead of looking for religious truth in propositions drawn from the text, experiential-expressivism looks for that truth in propositions about the pre-text. It must quest insatiably for the historical Jesus, or the Johannine community, or the Petrine faction at Corinth, because the truth about God is to be found in the experience of Jesus or Peter or the community of the Beloved Disciple. Form critic Joachim Jeremias must sift every layer of Jesus' parables, because he is looking for the "actual living voice of Jesus."[7]

At its best, the experiential-expressivist encounter with the Bible leads to serious confrontation with the historical particularity of the Bible. For example, Jesus' encounter with the Canaanite woman (Matthew 15:21-28) can be seen as a transformative experience, where the Messiah of the Jews first glimpses the possibility of a universal mission. The woman bests Jesus in a verbal joust. Jesus, who came to the "children" of Israel, not Gentile "dogs," is surprised and pleased to be upstaged by the woman's answer, "Even the dogs under the table eat the children's crumbs." He rewards her and comes away with a better opinion of both women and Gentiles. Under this interpretation, Jesus' initial treatment of the woman as a "dog" proves to be a straightforward example of prejudice we must transcend, as Jesus himself learned. The virtue of this interpretation is that it avoids tendentious explanations that try to put Jesus in a better light — that he was testing the woman's mettle, or kidding her, or that "dogs" meant cute little puppies. Anyone who has squirmed through such artful dodges can appreciate this candid interpretation.

At its worst, however, experiential-expressivism leads to credulous historical explanations that are far less probable than the harmonizing readings of fundamentalism. Thus the feeding of the five thousand (Mark 6:30-44 and parallels) becomes the miracle of sharing: when the people saw the example of the generous little boy who shared his five loaves and two fish, they all pulled from their knapsacks their hoarded sack lunches and shared with their neighbors. The almost obligatory appearance of the little boy, mentioned only in John, is perhaps due to sentimental reasons (it makes for a good children's sermon), but it shows that the experiential-expressivist will harmonize no less than the propositionalist. One seeks not to interpret the specific texts of Matthew, Mark, Luke, and John, but the underlying experience of Jesus and his followers. The rationalizing ploy will do, if it yields both explanation and sermon.

More sophisticated exegetes will turn from this kind of pseudo-historical reading and concentrate on the biblical texts themselves: Matthew will be read as Matthew's story, Mark for Mark's sake, Luke as Lukan. The presupposition that the text is underlaid by religious experience is not abandoned, but merely pushed to another level. It is not the experience of Jesus we are seeking to recover, but that of Matthew's community, or Mark's, or Luke's, or John's, or Paul's. The religious experience being sought is that of the community which preserved the text. This sort of interpretation was dominant in the critical guild for a long time and perhaps is still so today. Form criticism, which is the study of how and why various bits of biblical material were handed down, seeks to determine the *Sitz im Leben* ("situation in life") of the individual units that made up the Gospels; that *Sitz im Leben* consisted of the religious (usually liturgical) needs of the community which passed the tradition along. Redaction criticism, which is the study of the role of the editors of the traditional material found in the Gospels and other biblical texts, examines the way the individual units of biblical tradition were modified, in order to find clues about the religious experience of those who compiled the traditions. A more recent trend, canonical criticism, goes beyond redaction criticism's study of the changes made to this or that biblical saying or story to look at the broader process of compilation; it looks for the religious situation that prompted the assembly of widely divergent traditions into a single yet variegated text, and into a single yet diverse scripture.

The strangest legacy of historical-critical methods such as form and redaction criticism is that they leave the impression that biblical texts are vast allegories. In some critical views, for example, Luke-Acts does not portray a struggle between the Jewish hierarchy and upstart Jewish messianists; the real story is not about Jesus or Peter or Paul. The bad Jews of Luke's story stand for the Jewish Christians who are a hindrance to Luke's own Gentile community. The contest is not between Jesus and the Pharisees, nor Paul and the Council, but between Jewish and Gentile Christians of Luke's own day. Similarly, John's Gospel, with its ambiguous portrait of "the Jews," is really about early Jewish Christians thrown out of the synagogue. Likewise, statements made in Pauline epistles are taken as polemics against now-obscure enemies who assume the characteristics of someone who takes Paul's advice and does the exact opposite. Any Pauline (or post-Pauline) statement, no matter how formulaic, may become fodder for such a mirror reading. Thus the exhortation to avoid "old wives' tales" (1 Timothy 4:7), along with the instructions to widows (1 Timothy 5:3-16), are taken not as stock rhetorical flourishes but as a rearguard action against factions of rebellious unmarried women who have challenged apostolic tradition. This kind of scholarship is an easy target for parody: when Ephesians announces that "Thieves must give up stealing" (Ephesians 4:28), does this hint at the presence of an "Unrepentant Thieves Faction" in the Ephesian church? Where fundamentalism took the Bible as one large proposition, these critics see it as a collection of intricate allegories about then-current events. Interpretation again proceeds from presupposition; the quest for religious experience finds it in the seams of a multi-layered biblical text.

Experiential-expressivism in both its naive and sophisticated forms is prone to use psychologizing as a exegetical tool. "Psychologizing" imputes some sort of psychological motive to the authors or characters of a biblical text, but it is not usually the work of serious students of Freud or Jung. Oprah, Phil, and the other television tabloids indicate the extent to which we value understanding the pyschic and social forces that propel our behavior, and in an age when everyone is an armchair analyst, psychologizing proliferates in both pulpit and study. Understandably, many interpreters fill in the Bible's gaps with the pop psychology that proves so useful in other facets of life, no matter how far removed it is from the culture that produced the ancient text, and no matter how fanciful the presumed psychic motivation. The text can be explained if we discover the true motivation of either the historical Jesus or the church which told this story. Often the resulting psychological hypothesis becomes the pivot on which the sermon turns. The perennial "miracle of sharing" interpretation of the feeding of the five thousand substitutes psychology for miracle and makes it the point. In the same way, if we can determine why his friends brought the paralytic to Jesus, we can perhaps preach a sermon on it. The Markan text speaks of the pallet-bearers' "faith," presumably in Jesus (Mark 2:5), but the psychologizing preacher will not hesitate to draw lessons about their love, loyalty, and hope. The congregation may even become privy to the ineffective protests of the paralyzed man, who would rather not impose on these good people. The power of this tool is shown in that it works even on texts most repugnant to modern consciousness; once we know that Revelation was born out of the fears of a persecuted people, we can speak to the fears of our own congregation. Psychologizing comes as a natural tool for the experiential-expressivist, who seeks an explanation in human experience and cannot imagine that different humans have different experiences.

For all its attempts to make the Bible transparent to the modern mind, experiential-expressivism lacks a cogent homiletical reason for using the Bible at all. Why should the particular text assigned this morning reflect a laudable religious sentiment? Propositionalism in its fundamentalist form is at least consistent on this point; any biblical text could contain a Word from God, since all was uttered by God. But there is no inherent reason, once one has abandoned propositionalism, why any given text should yield an experience of God at all. There is further no guarantee that this experience, if found, will be relevant to the congregation, or even commendable.[8] Feminist biblical critics, for example, have shown that some biblical texts present violence against women as the norm; while we omit those texts from the Sunday rotation, we may find it hard to purge all texts of their negative cultural particularities, some of which are quite subtle.[9] No wonder that many preachers trained in experiential-expressivist theological models stick to the most congenial passages. Others virtually abandon the Bible in favor of more promising literature. The Sunday lection may or may not prove to contain a Word from God. It might be easier to find an appropriate Word in today's newspaper, a recent novel, or a children's story. All religious texts, and many secular texts, reflect the experience of the divine, which is the same for everyone.

Ultimately the experiential-expressive model becomes even more unsatisfactory in the pulpit than propositionalism. Under propositionalism, the preacher and the congregation can at least open a book and agree on what is said there. The experiential-expressivist who takes the task seriously must deliver a new text to the congregation, while trying to draw a message from that text. That text is the historical reconstruction of what underlay the biblical passage, the religious impulses at work in the creation of the Bible. To be successful at this kind of preaching, one must not only be an incredibly gifted biblical critic but also a creative, imaginative genius, able to bridge the gap between historical hypothesis and modern religious sentiment with grace, relevance, and charm, holding high both ancient and modern religious experience for all to see clearly. Chances are that for most of us, something will give between the two poles, and we will end up stranded on one side or the other. Only the most diligent of preachers can survive Sunday after Sunday under this herculean burden.

The Bible And "Religion Does"

Lindbeck's third way of viewing theological statements is the model he calls "cultural-linguistic," what I have called "Religion Does." Under this view the Bible is like a culture or a language in providing the basic foundation from which religious experience is constructed. A cultural-linguist sees the text neither as a series of propositions nor as mere expressions of religious sentiment, but as the building blocks of the faith. Biblical texts contribute their images, stories, poetry, history, instruction, and prophetic oracles to the world of symbols used by the religious community. These biblical elements contribute to the development of that community, much as language enables speech, or cultural etiquette enables smooth and harmonious social gatherings.

This is not to say that one may safely ignore propositions, which, true or false, are found in abundance in the Bible and in theology. Nor does the cultural-linguistic view deny that religious language may to some extent represent and be changed by the experiences of its users. The question is the way one leans, the primary emphasis. The cultural-linguist believes first of all in the power of symbols to create a world.

To be fair, the cultural-linguistic position is not without its potential pitfalls (as many critics of Lindbeck have pointed out). Some critics worry that the cultural-linguist may construe tradition's formative role in too restrictive a way; rather than becoming the foundation of a vibrant, living religious faith, the tradition becomes a conservative straightjacket, binding religious culture to a certain place and time, restricting all new innovation. Authoritarianism is the obvious by-product of this restrictive construal of the cultural-linguistic view.

However, to become doctrinaire and authoritarian would be to fall back into propositionalism. The cultural-linguist does not claim that religious tradition, biblical or otherwise, should be taken as unchanging and invariant. Quite the contrary, Lindbeck uses his theories in the context of ecumenical dialogue to show how doctrines, taken as the grammar or the cultural rules of religious faith, can change and yet remain the same. Thus one need not hold the metaphysics of medieval scholasticism to join in a liturgical recitation of the Nicene Creed. To say that Jesus is "one being with the Father" is to invoke thought patterns different from those it brought to mind in its original setting. Cosmology and anthropology — ways we speak of "being" — have changed significantly since then, and we are currently witnessing changes in the connotation of "Father." Yet underlying the very different ancient and modern readings of these words lie the same guidelines for understanding, like the rules of grammar which can be used to create many different sentences. In this case, to make sense of the Creed one must find some way to affirm certain tenets, which might be said to be "rules," such as monotheism, the historical particularity of Jesus, and the notion that Jesus is the highest revelation of God.[10]

In the sermon it is the texts themselves that interest the cultural-linguist, not their pre-history nor their distillation into a single proposition. Historical criticism is a useful and necessary tool for understanding a text. But criticism is not the subject of our preaching, because as a specialized language it is not a text we share with the church at large. It is the scriptures themselves which we share with our congregations and which form us together as a Christian community. The arguments, images, and stories of the Bible make us who we are.[11] As I shall argue later in this chapter, we have set up a particular way of construing these texts when we have designated them as "canon," and the implication for preaching is clear: we preach the texts as canon.

The advantage of the cultural-linguistic view is that it deals with the function of texts as texts. We are not reducing stories to propositions (as in propositionalism) nor probing behind the story for a historical lesson (as does the experiential-expressivist doing historical criticism). Under the cultural-linguistic view, we are reading a story as a story, not as a reconstructed event. Mark's version of the feeding of the five thousand is different from John's. Each stands in a different place in its respective plot. Each makes a different point. Mark emphasizes the disciples' growing understanding of Jesus' true nature. In John, the disciples are not so dense, but the people have difficulty understanding that Jesus offers a spiritual and not an earthly kingdom. The preacher who takes seriously these differences will not preach the same sermon on both texts. In the same way, the resurrection account in Matthew (Matthew 28:1-10) makes a different point from that of Mark (Mark 16:1-8) or Luke (Luke 24:1-12) or John (John 20:1-10). In congregations that use a lectionary, one expects to hear a different sermon at the Easter Vigil (when Matthew is read) from that of Easter Morning. Similarly, the Christmas Eve sermon on Luke 2 will not do on Christmas Day, when the prologue to John is read.

It will by now be obvious that in this book I am advocating a cultural-linguistic view of preaching. In my opinion a consistent cultural-linguistic position presents the fewest problems for dealing honestly with both Bible and human experience and opens up new ways for the preacher to understand the pulpit. It offers a way to make a critical reading of the biblical text (in my view, the only consistent reading) useful in the pulpit.

Reading Critically

But why use critical methods at all? Cannot the text function simply as text, without resort to elaborate theories about how it functions or when it came into being? Not if we are to take seriously the notion, developed in the last chapter, of the interpretive community. Texts are not uncomplicated entities that exist somewhere out there, untouched by space and time. Even if they were, we cannot treat them that way because we bring to any book presuppositions about texts and reading. Like interpretive communities, texts are beset with historical particularities.

Let me note that when I suggest that we must read critically, I do not mean that we must be historical skeptics. For some, critical study has come to mean that one denies that the events described in the Bible have any historical basis; one periodically sees in the newspaper the latest cleric who has announced that the Exodus, the virgin birth, or the resurrection could not have happened, according to "critical" scholarship. The critical approach must not be confused with historical skepticism, however; criticism allows for a variety of methods. Some critical methods may encourage historical skepticism, others may yield more positive evaluations, while still others have no interest in historical reconstruction whatever.

When I say that we must read critically, I mean that we must take both text and readers for what they are. In the history of biblical scholarship, a good deal of time has been spent trying to determine what kind of texts make up the Bible: their sources, their authors, their editors and keepers. It is impossible to read the text intelligently while ignoring this scholarship, because otherwise one is not playing fairly with the text. The scholarship shows the biblical text simply for what it is, a composite document assembled over a lengthy period of time by many different factions in a certain historical and religious tradition. It is not always consistent; it contains errors of fact and substance. It is neither a Ouija board nor an oracle, and it did not drop from heaven untouched by human hands.

If we are honest about the text, we must also be honest about ourselves. As we saw in the last chapter, recent trends in literary criticism and biblical scholarship have made it clear that no reader can approach the text without presuppositions about it. In some sense, we cannot avoid reading critically because we always put the text through a sieve. When we read we do not act as impartial observers: we want something from these writings — a sermon, a devotional thought, a glimpse of history, or even simple amusement. The critical reader recognizes both the text as it is and as the reader would like it to be.

This is perhaps to say that the critical reader recognizes the irony of reading: one must see clearly while wearing colored glasses. Or it is perhaps simply to say that one must read honestly. It is a matter of honesty to acknowledge one's own presuppositions, just as it is a matter of honesty to read a text for what it is rather than what it is not. If the interpreter must become a tightrope walker, so be it. The tightrope walker at least makes a habit of care and accuracy.

Critical methods help us read the Bible with care and accuracy. They refine our skills at reading. Exegesis, however fuzzy a concept to seminarians, is little more than a very careful reading of a text. The point of learning this or that critical method, of mastering the skills involved in redaction criticism or source analysis, is to learn to read more thoroughly and carefully. Biblical scholarship over the years has developed powerful tools for the careful sifting of words. If a critical method helps us refine our reading skills, there is no reason not to use it. If a new method yields fruit only reluctantly or not at all, we best first become more skilled practitioners before abandoning it.

We are all to some degree critical readers, whether we know it or not, because we are all members of certain interpretive communities. Even to take up a translation is to perform a critical act, since every translation is an interpretation. One who raises *The New International Version* makes a different critical judgment than the one who lifts *The New Revised Standard Version*, though both act less critically than the preacher who takes up both versions. This third preacher recognizes that one of the simplest ways of reading with care is to compare several translations. For example, the reader of *The New Revised Standard* will see that in Mark 6:48 Jesus walked on the water "early in the morning." To stop there is to understand, at least somewhat — but was it 9:00 a.m., light outside, or 4:00 a.m., completely dark? The critical reader turns to *The Jerusalem Bible* and finds a puzzle: the time is "the fourth watch of the night"; when exactly was that? The puzzle is solved by reference to *Today's English Version*, which puts the time at "sometime between three and six o'clock in the morning." One may conclude (without reference to a Bible dictionary or commentary) that the fourth watch referred to this time period, and thus one has performed a critical act. The unfortunate reader who consults only one of these translations has a less comprehensive, and therefore less accurate, understanding. Examples like this can be multiplied by the thousands, and not just concerning relatively minor points of chronology.

A critical reading of the text is simply a careful, honest reading. In this same section of Mark (Mark 6:45-52), Jesus takes his pre-dawn stroll across the sea of Galilee, sees the disciples straining against a fierce wind, and bids the wind to cease. The story may seem on first reading to be a rescue story: the disciples are having trouble with the boat, and Jesus comes to save them. Mark, however, does not say that the disciples are under any threat; they are simply unable to make any headway against the wind (v. 48). Besides, if the point is a rescue, how can one explain the strange statement that "he intended to pass them by" (v. 48)? A psychologizing interpreter may dismiss the remark; perhaps Jesus was preoccupied with the events of the day. The critical reader will suspect that there is more going on here, recognizing that such stories about Jesus were heavily influenced by the narratives of the Hebrew Bible. When the Markan passage is read in light of its Old Testament allusions, the suspicion is borne out. The first clue (accessible to those who read Greek) is found in Jesus' words of encouragement to the disciples, "Take heart; it is I," which could be translated literally, "Take heart; I am" (Greek *ego eimi*). Here is, possibly, an allusion to the Divine Name spoken from the burning bush to Moses (Exodus 3:13-15). Could the Markan Jesus be obliquely claiming divine origin? Now the quizzical statement about Jesus' intent to pass them may be seen in a different light; it too may be an allusion to the Moses story. In a veiled theophany, God passed by to present a fleeting view of divine glory, allowing Moses to see only the trailing end of God's presence, thus sheltering him from the sure death of seeing God face-to-face (Exodus 33:18-23). Here in Mark is Jesus, himself proclaiming "I am," showing the disciples a brief glimpse of divinity. Mark writes not about a rescue but a theophany, as the disciples catch a glimpse of a mysterious, otherworldly Jesus passing them in the night.[12] The genius is that Mark suggests rather than dictates; he subtly alludes to what the disciples are not ready to state, perhaps producing in the reader much the same confusion as the disciples experienced (vv. 50-52). The story thus interpreted fits well in Mark's plot, which is telling of the disciples' nascent understanding of who Jesus is: they do not understand (cf. v. 51), but God isn't finished with them yet (a similar story, at a further point in the plot development, is found in Mark 9:2-8). Uncritical and superficial study of this passage will lead to a sermon about Jesus saving us from the storms of life; a more careful reading produces a somewhat different emphasis and a more profound and befuddling Jesus.

This is not scholarly nitpicking; it is a matter of our integrity as preachers and our claim to be telling the truth. We can ill afford to sacrifice our credibility by playing fast and loose with the truth, particularly with the truth about the Bible. The preacher who wrestles seriously in the study can at least stand in the pulpit with the assurance that she has met the text and lived; if she is both diligent and lucky, she has learned something from the experience. What if no one should notice but the preacher? Congregations come and go, but a conscience is lived with always.

As we have already seen, all texts have "gaps" which must be filled in by the reader. One of the glories of biblical scholarship through the years is the diverse variety of devices that have been invented for gap-filling. Once we stop looking for the one-and-only-one propositional meaning of a text, or the foundational experience underlying a text, we are free to explore how the various methods of scriptural interpretation can open up the text in meaningful ways — how the symbolic world of the Bible can come into and transform our world. Pre-critical and uncritical methods such as spiritual reading and allegorical interpretation may have important roles in the life of faith and even in sermon preparation, but critical methods offer proven ways to render a careful, thoughtful reading.

Reading Otherness

Simple honesty is a laudable and necessary reason for practicing critical biblical interpretation, but there are deeper and more profound reasons for reading critically. We need to read in this way because of who we are, or to be more accurate, who God is and who we are before God. I would suggest that there is a *theological* reason for being the best critical readers we can be. I use the word "theological" in the best and most profound sense of that term: we read a certain way because we believe in a certain kind of

God. To read critically is, I will argue, to read theologically. It is to get at the Other in the otherness of the biblical text.[13]

Divine And Human Otherness

As Christians, we believe certain things about God. We believe, for example, that God is Creator, and we are created. Traditionally, we have understood this to mean that God as a creative force is continually sustaining our world; were God to remove the creative hand, we and all that we take for granted would cease to exist. God is not the watchmaker who wound the thing and walked away, but one in whom we continually live and move and have our being. As such, God is also our Judge. The concept of God as Judge has often come under attack, but if we see God's role of Judge as an extension of the role of Creator, we need not picture a deity of arbitrary whims, dangling human beings by a thread over eternal fire. Rather, God is Judge because as the one who created and continually sustains us, God knows us best and sees us truly. We may deceive ourselves, we may be oblivious of some aspects of our lives, but God knows exactly who we are. God is the only impartial observer. Also following from the concept of God as Creator is the idea that God is the only Savior. As creations, we are absolutely dependent on God. Should we need rescue (from ourselves or from an outside force), only the one who made us has ultimate power. Similarly, if there is any hope of our changing, it is the God who created us who must grant that power. Thus we speak of God as a transforming power, God as Sanctifier.

All of these statements about God — that God is Creator, Judge, Savior, and Sanctifier — have important implications for us as human beings; with the theological truth comes a corresponding anthropological truth. To proclaim that God is Creator is to assert that we do not create ourselves and do not have ultimate control over ourselves. To say that God is Judge means that we do not see ourselves impartially and without self-deception. To proclaim God as Savior is to confess our inability to save ourselves. To call God Sanctifier is to admit that in our feebleness as created beings we cannot substantially change ourselves. In short, we are human, God is divine; we are created, God is the source of all being. We are not

God. This is what theologians mean when they speak of the "absolute qualitative difference between God and humanity." The difference may be summed up simply: God is Other.

Perhaps the most amazing capacity of the human beings created by this Other is our ability to choose. We humans are created with freedom. Unlike other animals, who live in predetermined patterns programmed by instinct, we must choose how to live. The choices are vast. Shall I live in this town or that? Shall I take job one or job two? A whole range of choices lies before us from birth to death — not unlimited choices, it is true, since we are limited by a host of factors, physical, social, political, and economic. Still, we are free to choose from a wide range of human activity. I may no longer, at age 36, have the option of becoming a professional baseball player; given my weak knees, it may have never been a feasible option. But on more than 100 days in a year I can choose to go to the ballpark, or watch the game on television, or play catch with the neighborhood kids. Or I may choose to forget baseball altogether, and concentrate on my work. We are created with a certain amount of freedom. The Other has made us this way, for reasons God alone knows — but then, if discipleship is to make any sense, we must be able to choose whether to follow this God.

As a result of our freedom, individual humans are substantially different from one another. We all have physical differences, being bodily creatures. Yet our variations are greater because of our freedom; if we had been created to live only by predetermined patterns, our differences would be extremely limited — we may look different, but we would all have the same personalities, like ducks with different coats who nevertheless all walk and quack like ducks. As it is, we have different personalities and varying psychologies. We are raised in different social settings; we come from different cultures. One group of humans went this way and made things so; another went that way and made things thus. My choice to play baseball in the summers during high school meant I had less spending money than my friends who worked at the mall; we had different values and chose accordingly. My ancestors' choice to move to America meant that I would be playing baseball and not cricket.

We see things differently. Our freedom as a species to move and choose has made it so.

Our human freedom has a negative side in that it leaves us no inherent anchor for our lives. We must determine our own standards of life, our own values and beliefs. Lacking any innate guide or outside influence, we tend to take the easiest path. We take our own desires and center our lives on them. In short, we take the relative for absolute. The biblical word for this is "idolatry," which does not simply refer to the worship of stone and wood figures, but to the human tendency to substitute the created for the Creator. We all have idolatrous impulses which we tend to make into an idolatrous way of life. Being free creatures and having no predetermined foundation, we tend to seek meaning in what is obviously available in the created world — food, sex, money, power, and so on. We build our lives based on the available choices and, lacking any obstacles to the free exercise of our will, life goes on according to plan. Given no interference from the outside, I am free to make absolute any created thing and to construct an entire life around it. Of course, by doing so, I actually and ironically make myself a slave, since no created thing, not food, sex, money, nor power, can bear the burden of divinity. (Witness the proliferation of Alcoholics-, Narcotics-, and Overeaters Anonymous, along with various other twelve-step programs, not to mention the self-help shelves at the bookstore and the electronic confessional booth staffed by Oprah, Donahue, and their ilk.)

Fortunately salvation comes from the outside. Because I do not act in a vacuum, my particular expression of idolatry will soon encounter a very serious obstacle. That obstacle is you. While I was busy constructing my idolatrous life, you were equally hard at work constructing one of your own. My plan may not jibe with your plan. As we live out these plans, inevitably obstacles — the plans and choices of other human beings — will cross our paths. If I want to be District Manager, you cannot be. If I want to marry Susie, she cannot marry Jack. Our freedom can and frequently does clash with the freedom of other human beings. Though these clashes may be painful, they are opportunities for experiencing grace. They remind us that we are not in charge but owe our existence to an

Other. Seen as pinprick reminders of our joint dependence on God, our colliding idolatries present a challenge to live not for ourselves but for that Other. Which means, on a human level, to live for others, and to be other for them. Whenever we experience the power of otherness, we are at some basic level experiencing the pull of Otherness.

Thus the implication of our human freedom is that, to some extent, we confront in each other a glimpse of the divine. We are other, small "o," to one another, simply by virtue of our existence. When I meet you, I am met by something outside myself. You are other to me. You may not play baseball, you may not have grown up in America, you may not write books about preaching. Even if we are similar, we are in a thousand ways different. As other, you remind me that I am not in charge — I did not create myself nor you, I do not see either of us with true clarity, and I have no power to change or save either of us. I cannot control you, because you exercise freedom of choice independently of my will. Your presence as other reminds me that I am not God. Presumably I do the same for you. The other, small "o," testifies to the existence of Other, large "O." Human otherness is a means of encountering the Otherness of God. Otherness is in fact God's gift of grace, as it reminds us that we owe our existence to the One who is not us. Our lifelong journey of faith is the process of recognizing and accepting God's gift of grace as we encounter it in the other.

Luke T. Johnson, whose thinking on spirituality I have been recounting, gives this analogy for the process of realigning one's life around an Other.[14] Suppose a young man momentarily spies a pretty face in the stacks of the college library. A chord resounds deep inside, and he runs to the end of the aisle where he saw her. Nothing. He runs to the elevators, but again nothing. He goes back to the dorm, but he cannot get the fleeting image out of his mind. The other, however ineffable, has tremendous power over him; he finds himself blushing in the middle of a lecture, thinking of her, unable to concentrate on anything. He rearranges his schedule so that he can be in that part of the library again at the same time the next day, and the next day, and the next. He has in fact reorganized his whole life on the basis of that fleeting encounter with an other.

Perhaps his efforts will be in vain, and the face will never reappear; still, his life is different because he has been called out of himself. Perhaps, however, they will meet, perhaps fall in love, perhaps marry — how completely a life can be changed based on that fleeting encounter with otherness!

So too the religious experience of encountering the Other rearranges life. In particular, it calls us to see in each other that glimpse of otherness and to recognize together that we are not our own, but belong to our Creator. Fellow creatures and servants of that Creator, we devote ourselves to one another, as our encounter with each other provides the surest glimpse of our ultimate hope. In opening ourselves to an other, any other, we drop for a moment our own idolatrous impulses. We think not of our own desires but of the wishes of another. The other person impinging on my life has in fact given me a gift, allowing me to see my own idolatry for what it is. My plans are not ultimate; I owe my life elsewhere. The life of faith is a continual process of opening ourselves to God's grace which comes through the gift of otherness. We learn, over time, to open our selves and use our freedom to choose the good of the other.

Otherness And The Biblical Text

I would suggest that the otherness of human beings which is but a sign of divine Otherness cannot be limited to the flesh-and-blood creatures with whom we come into contact on a day-to-day basis. Human beings have many different ways of communicating, and any means of communication can convey the voice of the other to us — books, letters, phone calls, movies, and even television shows. This means that the other need not be physically present with us in order to grace us with otherness. The other need not even be still living. For Johnson, the ultimate model of the one who gave himself for others is Jesus himself, and Jesus is known only through reading the biblical texts.

Biblical texts, I contend, provide a particularly vivid sense of the other, and they do so best when read critically. It is not just that the subject of the Bible, by and large, is the presence of the Other. These texts by their very nature confront us with otherness. They come from a different place and time. They were written in societies which had different modes of communication from our own, with very particular rules about how one goes about saying something. They were compiled, edited, and added to by successive generations, all living and working in changing situations. This otherness is uncovered by a critical reading, which provides tools to sift through the various layers of the text and place them in historical and literary perspective. To read without critical method is to skim the surface, perhaps finding only what one already knew was there. Without criticism, the Bible is simply a mirror, reflecting the face of the reader. Historical and literary critical study helps us see the other in the text.

The otherness of God is reflected in the otherness of a historical text. The Bible, studied in its historical and literary context, is a primary source of otherness. Its thoughts, stories, images, and symbols bring the other into our lives. As we immerse ourselves in the thoughts, images, and stories of its world, we assume its characteristic otherness. Discerning and reflecting on this otherness, we come into touch with the Other, capital "O."

For example, picture the preacher preparing to preach a sermon on 1 Corinthians 10:1-13. The preacher reads the text and fixes on v. 13: "No temptation has overtaken you that is not common to man. God is faithful, and he will not let you be tempted beyond your strength, but with the temptation will also provide the way of escape, that you may be able to endure it" (RSV). A little meditation, and a sermon on "temptation" takes shape — a few dramatic stories about tempting situations, the good news that Jesus gives us a way out, and an exhortation to rely on him in the midst of temptation. With a little rhetorical flair, it might produce an interesting sermon. (I actually heard such a sermon once, and it was interesting.) But it is all too easy.

So our preacher, duly trained in critical method and knowing that the process of discovering the Other has just begun, will first of all consult another translation, which (if it is the NRSV) will use the word "testing" rather than "temptation." "Testing," of course, does not have the same connotation in English as "temptation," so the digging begins. It soon becomes clear that the verse is a generalization based on some specific examples drawn from the Old Testament: the stories of the Exodus and Israel in the Wilderness. "Our ancestors were all under the cloud," says Paul, "and all passed through the sea," (v. 1) that is, they were led by God, who appeared in a pillar of cloud, out of Egypt and through the Red Sea. In the wilderness, they "all ate the same spiritual food," and all "drank from the spiritual rock" (vv. 3-4): they ate manna from heaven, and Moses produced water from a rock. Still, "God was not pleased with most of them" (v. 5) because they became idolaters, indulged in sexual immorality, and generally grumbled (vv. 7-10). "These things happened," says Paul, "to instruct us" (v. 11). He concludes, "So if you think you are standing, watch out that you do not fall" (v. 12). The implication is that just as Israel was tested in the wilderness, and many proved to fall short of God's standards, so too the Corinthians are not immune to a fall.

At this point, our preacher could still go back and preach the temptation sermon, adding the story of Israel in the wilderness to the stock of modern stories in order to give the sermon more biblical flavor. But again, the preacher is too well trained to stop now. Besides, an intriguing question has risen: what is it about the Corinthians that Paul would use this example? Is he speaking of temptation in a general way, or is there some specific subject in his mind? The question is answered by the study of the context. The preacher reads on beyond the lection to the next verse: "Flee from the worship of idols," says Paul (v. 14). This passage, the preacher realizes, is about idols. Further reading shows that the entire section, 1 Corinthians 8-10, is devoted to the subject of idolatry — specifically, the controversy over meat offered to idols (cf. 8:4). A quick look at a Bible dictionary or a commentary will reveal that pagan temples served as slaughterhouses, the leftover meat ending up in the marketplaces. At times it may have been hard to find fresh meat that was not used in a pagan ritual. For the Christians at Corinth, this raised a problem: is it permissible to eat such meat, or has it been tainted by idol worship? Some said that meat was meat, idols are mere wood and stone. Being strong in Christ, a Christian was in no danger from such meat. Others, however, were not so sure. Paul begins by agreeing with the first group, that idols do not exist (1 Corinthians 8:4-6). However, he exhorts this group not to let their knowledge get in the way of their love; they are not to eat such meat if it disturbs the faith of "those weak believers" who still worry about idols (8:7-13). He reinforces his exhortation with his own example: though he is an apostle, he does not stand by his rights, but lives for others (chapter 9). Now he comes to the negative example of Israel in the wilderness (10:1-13) and gives a passionate exhortation against the participation in the pagan rituals themselves, asserting that the powers behind idol worship are demonic — idols are not inert, but are actually demons (10:16-22). He then adds further cautions about the idol meat available in the marketplace (10:23-33). The implications of the preacher's lectionary passage now become clear: Paul is warning those who think they are strong enough to eat idol meat not to take too much for granted. Israel, though it experienced the pinnacle of God's saving grace, still fell into idolatry. Take care, Paul seems to say, lest you too be misled into thinking you are immune from idolatrous, demonic forces.

Now more things about the lection fall into place. The examples of Israel's sin, it turns out, all have to do with idolatry. The first involves the worship of golden calf (10:7, cf. Exodus 32:1-6). The reference to "sexual immorality" refers to the episode where Israelite men took Moabite wives and began to worship their gods (v. 8, cf. Numbers 25:1-9). The people's complaining questioned God's provision and thus put human desires before God's (v. 10, cf. Numbers 16:13-14, 41-49). Paul's use of Israel as an example was completely appropriate to the Corinthian situation. Though the people of Israel were in a strong position, or thought they were, they still succumbed to idolatry. The Corinthians should not forget how weak and fickle human nature is. We have not arrived at faith but are in a process of being faithful and still prone to substitute the partial for the Whole. God's people are by the nature of things constantly testing their faith, for there are always temptations to idolatry. Paul's solemn warning to the Corinthians concludes with the promise of God's help in the midst of this testing.

All this suggests that the preacher preparing a sermon on this text will not look for generalized examples of temptation or testing.

The focus has become much more clear: it is idolatry. The preacher may want to explore the ways idolatry manifests itself in modern life, perhaps looking for the ways in which we modern people think that we have it made but are in danger of a fall. What does it mean to live a life of faith, for example, in a town where you are judged by where your house is located, but hurricanes could easily flatten all the houses? I leave it to the preacher to spin out the rest of the sermon. My point is that between the first superficial and the later critical reading, the interpretive category has changed. The finished sermon is not about temptation but idolatry.

The preacher thus arrives at a sermon because it presents him with something he did not know. It has been a very strange journey into a very strange world, where animals are sacrificed in religious rituals, where temples sell stock to grocery stores, where demons lurk behind every corner. I do not even mention Paul's exegetical method, which allows him to see Christ as the rock following Israel in the desert (10:4, 9). These ideas, this culture, is so foreign to our way of life that it may be difficult even to find a modern analogy to the ancient situation. It is a very strange world the preacher enters when reading a biblical text carefully. This world is filled with otherness.

The irony of the critical reading process is that getting to the utter irrelevance of the historical text enables this text to speak relevantly to our time. Particularity yields universalism, because to step out of ourselves long enough to see the other as it truly is allows us to turn and look back from the outside, as it were. Seeing the other gives us a different perspective on ourselves. The text makes us relative. It shows our everyday concerns to be exactly what, in the long run, they are: temporary, parochial, and ultimately idolatrous. The preacher who reads critically reaches back into the text and pulls out something quite other. The preacher is him- or herself confronted with the graceful gift of otherness. The text yields not what we already knew, but something foreign. It calls us out of ourselves, reminding us that the world does not revolve around us, and that God has been at work in a variety of situations. It questions our idolatrous worship of all things modern by showing us that God was at work before the computer, before the typewriter, even before the printing press. The critical reading of the text confronts us with another way of piecing together the puzzle of God's work in the world. Insofar as it does all this, it calls us out of idolatry and towards the Other.

"I do not want to scatter pearls of wisdom from the pulpit," says Barbara Brown Taylor, "I want to discover something fresh — even if I cannot quite identify it yet, even if it is still covered with twigs and mud."[15] The critical reading of these texts — reading them carefully and honestly for what they are, and in light of who we are — helps us discover things we could never learn by ourselves. Most of all, by stressing the historical and literary context of biblical passages, critical reading helps preserve that sense of otherness which is so crucial to understanding our place in creation.

Reading Canonically

Why, then, these texts and not some other? True, the preacher will read other texts and find otherness there. A story from the week's news, a Zen parable, or a one-liner from Groucho Marx, all may be a gift of grace for the people, and the preacher will use them and more. Biblical texts, however, are in the judgment of the church canonical; they are foundational, and they are most likely to yield the religious truth for which we are looking. These are the documents that have brought and still bring the church into being. Canon and church live together; they imply each other. The church needs the canon to bring it into being, just as the canon could not exist apart from the church. The church recognizes in these texts its own beginnings and its ongoing life as it listens to them in the liturgy, week after week. The church keeps the canon alive because the canon keeps the church alive. These texts have formed and continue to form the community, precisely because they communicate the God who is Other; and it is this God, we believe, who has called both community and canon into being.

There is no magic in the canon. "Canon" simply means "measure," and the body of canonical literature is that by which the church has traditionally measured itself. It cannot be added to or changed, not by any new documents ancient or modern, otherwise the measure would no longer be the same measure. The canon is the common denominator of the church, the texts shared by each successive generation of believers. Through the ages, these texts taken as a whole have been judged to yield the voice of God. To listen to them is to join with the faithful of all ages. By affirming the canon, the church asserts its continuity with the church of every age gone by. It is the same church because it shares the same canon. That the canon has persisted shows not only that these writings persistently generate meaning, but that the church persists with the canon and because of it.

The canonical writings provide the symbolic world which has brought the church into being. This means that the texts themselves, not our critical theories about them, are the foundation of our faith and the material of the sermon. The church as a whole and through the ages does not share the various critical hypotheses about authorship, date, and redaction. As I have shown, that kind of critical information is quite useful for the preacher who wishes to understand the text. Insofar as it helps us interpret the canonical text, critical reading is essential. But it is not in and of itself the basis of the sermon.

The canon is, of course, a diverse body of texts, and that is the point. The church does not recognize just one literary piece as the Word of God. The canon includes not just the five books of Moses, but the prophetic critique of life under the Mosaic Law. The prescriptive wisdom of Proverbs stands alongside the poetry of Job. There is not one gospel but four; the church rejected Tatian's *Diatessaron*, which harmonized the four into one narrative. The New Testament includes not just story but correspondence, and books such as Revelation combine a number of different literary forms. The biblical books differ from one another in form and content, and yet the church has through the ages proclaimed them as one canon. This diverse canon allows the church to enter into a wide-ranging conversation with itself. The various literary forms and viewpoints yield differing conclusions, as shown by the history of Christian conflict. One can find biblical support for many sides of one issue and argue accordingly. This is not a bad thing, if we recognize that the diversity of canon invites such an interpretive process. A number of differing positions can be read by the interpretive community, which then must engage together in a process of discerning God's truth. If the church is no monolith, it is because it does not measure itself by a monolithic canon. This very diversity allows the canon to speak compellingly in each new age. As Johnson puts it, "It is precisely in those elements of plurality and even disharmony that the texts open to new meanings, so that they are allowed to speak to the disharmonies and disjunctions of contemporary life."[16]

To step back a bit, I have argued that the encounter with the biblical text is one example of the human encounter with otherness, in which we experience a glimpse of the Other. Faced with a choice between our own idolatrous impulses and the impulses of an other, we open ourselves to God's grace. We do not, of course, always choose properly, nor is it always readily apparent which choice is proper — the serpent, after all, was "other" to Adam and Eve, but not in itself a means of grace. Your making your wishes known to me does not in and of itself constitute God's call to me, because your wishes may be self-centered, self-deceived, or otherwise misled — in short, you have your idolatrous impulses, and they are no better than mine. But my contact with you, and my decision about whether to follow you, forces me to consider at least for a moment the call of the Other. Johnson uses this example[17]: suppose I have a young daughter, and just as I sit down to watch my Saturday afternoon baseball game on television, I hear her call from the next room, "Daddy, come play with me." I may decide to go play, or I may decide that my own wishes override hers in this instance. If I never respond to her requests, however, I will soon find a daughter grown and independent who rarely visits; I will have deprived myself of her otherness. If I always capitulate, I will find myself inundated with requests to play, or for ice cream, or to have friends over — I am in danger of raising a spoiled brat! She has her idolatrous impulses, and I have mine; if either dominates, we are both deprived. I must engage in a very difficult task of discernment: which course of action is best for her and for me? There is no easy, pat answer, only the never ending process of listening and discerning, of hearing both my voice and the voice of one outside me. We must be other to one another, each relativizing the other's idolatrous impulses. The process is what keeps the relationship meaningful on both sides: she is daughter to me, and I am father to her. Over a lifetime, if I both listen to her otherness, and offer her my own, I become more and more open to my daughter. By implication, I have become more and more open to God.

In reading the Bible, as with any confrontation with human otherness, one must distinguish between the other's idolatry and the grace of God. The call of a biblical passage requires discernment no less than the call of the preacher's daughter from the next room: is this the voice of God or merely an invitation to join another's self-willed idolatry? The reader must distinguish between what William Placher calls "the true scandal of the cross and the false scandal of the sacrifice of the intellect."[18] Biblical texts, for one thing, do not always mesh well; Paul and James sit, albeit uncomfortably, in the same room, but Revelation would certainly be an interloper there, to say nothing of Leviticus. Some parts of the Bible modern people find difficult to believe; demons, water-walking, loaves and fishes, if accepted at all, are relegated to a special place that floats above normal life. Other biblical passages, filled with apparent anti-Semitism or the denigration of women, seem at odds with what the Spirit is saying to the churches. To believe in the Bible as a source of God's grace is to believe that it confronts us with both faith and idolatry, the human and the divine. It is not to accept every biblical notion without discernment (not even propositionalism does so). To read the text as other is to enter into a dialogue with many different voices, some but not all of which call us to faithful response. As with a living being, the reader relativizes the idolatrous impulses of the text, as the text does the same for the reader.

This principle is well illustrated by the ongoing debate over the role of women in the church. There is a good deal of New Testament material that prohibits the leadership of women in congregations (for example, 1 Corinthians 14:34-36; 1 Timothy 2:12-15). It is extremely hard to explain these commands away. One may dodge Paul's exhortation to female silence in 1 Corinthians by attributing it to a redactor but in so doing may feel somewhat like a sideshow magician ("Watch me pull a redactor out of my hat!"). 1 Timothy, however, remains in the canon even if it is held to be post-Pauline; as a canonical document its authority cannot be so easily dismissed. But the canonical prejudice against women is not entirely unanimous. Indeed, Paul seems to contradict himself in 1 Corinthians, since he pictures women praying and prophesying in public (1 Corinthians 11:5). In Galatians, Paul depicts a more egalitarian Christian society: "There is no longer Jew or Greek, there is no longer slave or free, there is no longer male or female; for all of you are one in Christ Jesus" (Galatians 3:28). It is hard to see how all can be one in Christ if half are denied the privileges and responsibilities of the other half. The canon is not monolithic; not even the Pauline tradition agrees with itself. Faced with the contradiction, we may argue one way or another, but our reasons for choosing this or that position have nothing to do with the texts themselves. The interpretive community, for its own good reasons, will prefer one reading over another. There is no guidance within the canon itself for choosing to stress Galatians 3 over 1 Timothy 2 — the reasons have to do with us as readers. If this seems too arbitrary, it is perhaps because we look for certainty in the wrong places, forgetting the role of the Spirit who leads us into all truth.

We do not always agree with every text. We exercise discernment. In some texts we find no antidote to our own idolatry, and in others we find a worse idolatry than our own. The stories of the rape of Tamar, the dismemberment of the Levite's concubine, or the presumed immolation of Jephthah's daughter do not find a place in our children's storybooks (2 Samuel 13:1-22; Judges 19:1-30; Judges 11:29-40). While we may at times share the psalmist's wish that our enemies' children be dashed against the rocks (Psalm 137:9), we will in our good moments remember Jesus' command to love our enemies as ourselves. Amos is often taken by preachers as a counter-culture hero, upholding justice over greed and selfishness. Which, of course, he is, but he may also be typical of one who would bring a system down with nothing but good intentions to replace it, and we may well be wary of some reforms proclaimed in his name. The Spirit can work with a "No" as well as a "Yes," and this is no less true because one is reading the Bible.

This sort of canon invites us to take all the more seriously the notion of the interpretive community. If the Bible is to function among us as the Word of God, it requires us to sit thoughtfully while listening for that Word. We read together with the church through the ages, but we also read now and in our own community. The preacher in particular reads with and for a certain community, the local church. If that community, and the larger entity of which it is a part, faces the issues of women's leadership, or racism, or crime and punishment, do we preachers not owe it the opportunity to sit under the various biblical witnesses, to read with them, to argue with them, to tell our own stories of how we see God at work in our lives? With practice, we might all become better at discerning the Spirit.

The interpretive community reading together discerns the call of God in the text. As preachers, we preach a text shared with the congregation and the church through the ages. Critical method allows us to stand back and see it for what it is, and this is essential, but in this interpretive community, it is the text itself which does its work on us. That work is simply to form a community, the church. The Bible is canon because it forms the church. Preaching is biblical when it lets the Bible loose to do that work among a congregation.

Conclusion

I have argued that biblical texts provide a necessary foundation for the formation of the Christian community. As the bedrock of our symbolic world, they help make us who we are. Preaching biblical texts thus requires serious engagement on the part of the preacher with these texts. Theologically, these texts as texts grace us by coming from a foreign time and place, thus confronting us with an otherness that points in some small way to the Other who made us. By designating these texts and no others as canon, the church through the ages testifies to their continuing importance in the formation of who we are as the people of God.

This does not mean, however, that the sermon itself is about the critical study of the Bible. In the last chapter, I indicated that I do not think that the language of critical biblical studies is appropriate for the pulpit; the interpretive community in which the preacher works has a different ethos and vocabulary from that of the average congregation, and the two will not mix easily. In this chapter I have further argued that the biblical texts as canon form the church by providing the source of its symbolic world. The texts themselves, not the methods we use to study them, are the foundation of the faith.

The preacher straddles two different interpretive communities and works in two different ways. The process of determining a message differs from the process of delivering it because the audience is different. Thus there are two steps in the making of a sermon: deciding what to say and deciding how to say it. In the first step the interpretive community is the world of biblical scholarship and theological reflection, and the audience is a member of that community, the preacher herself. In the second step, the audience has changed and so requires that the message take on a different form.

Getting to the Other is thus only half the battle. The preacher must take what has been discovered there out of the text and back to the congregation. Only then can it create a new world among the hearers.

---

1. Søren Kierkegaard, *Either/Or*, trans. David and Lillian Swenson (Garden City: Anchor Books, Doubleday, 1959), p. 1:281, quoted in Fred B. Craddock, *Overhearing the Gospel,* Beecher Lectures, 1978 (Nashville: Abingdon Press, 1978), p. 12.

2. Craddock, *Preaching*, p. 123.

3. Harry Emerson Fosdick, "Personal Counseling and Preaching," in Richard Lischer, *Theories of Preaching: Selected Readings in the Homiletical Tradition* (Durham: Labyrinth Press, 1987), p. 294.

4. I must note at this point that in simplifying Lindbeck's categories to "Religion Thinks," "Religion Feels," and "Religion Does," I do not wish to imply that these positions focus singlemindedly on one aspect of human perception. All the positions account for thinking, feeling, and doing, and at any point one may put an emphasis on propositions, experience, or customs — this is not what I am talking about. Nor can the three positions be harmonized into a single whole with different emphases. In each case the verb, "thinks," "feels," or "does," will have to be seen as a focal point or filter through which all else is seen. Each position is distinct not so much in emphasis but as a way of understanding (in technical terms, the thinking, feeling, and doing are "heuristic categories"). One cannot change willy-nilly between propositionalism and experiential-expressivism or cultural-linguism without massive confusion; they are distinct outlooks that exclude each other. The propositionalist sees all else through the filter of "I think that ..."; the experiential-expressivist sees all through experience or feeling, and the cultural-linguist view thinks of religion in terms of what it does.

5. This argument is made by Harold Lindsell, *The Battle for the Bible* (Grand Rapids: Zondervan, 1976), pp. 174-176.

6. See James Barr, *Fundamentalism* (Philadelphia: Westminster Press, 1977), and William H. Shepherd, Jr., "Revelation and the Hermeneutics of Dispensationalism," *Anglican Theological Review* 71 (1989), pp. 281-299.

7. Joachim Jeremias, *The Parables of Jesus,* trans. S. H. Hooke, second revised ed. (New York: Scribner's, 1972), p. 114.

8. On this point see Edward Farley, "Preaching the Bible and Preaching the Gospel," *Theology Today* 51 (1994), pp. 90-103. I will discuss Farley's argument in greater depth in the last chapter.

9. For example, Phyllis Trible, *Texts of Terror: Literary-Feminist Readings of Biblical Narratives* (Philadelphia: Fortress Press, 1984), and Elisabeth Schüssler Fiorenza, *Bread Not Stone: The Challenge of Feminist Biblical Interpretation* (Boston: Beacon Press, 1984).

10. See Lindbeck, *The Nature of Doctrine*, pp. 92-96.

11. I differ from Lindbeck in that I am not willing to lump the entire Bible into the single category "narrative" (see Lindbeck, *The Nature of Doctrine*, pp. 120-121). The diverse writings of scripture resist the artificial imposition of unity from the outside; certainly it is a stretch to speak of it all as narrative. The canon is distorted if one literary aspect subsumes the whole.

12. A further examination of the text will confirm this interpretation via source analysis: many scholars believe that Mark has combined two stories here, a theophany and a rescue story, the seams showing in vv. 48 and 51. The theophany story, however, dominates. The preacher who recognizes the combination of sources will not be tempted to elevate the clearly submerged rescue story over the theophany.

13. The argument that follows is obviously and profoundly indebted to Luke T. Johnson, *Faith's Freedom: A Classic Spirituality for Contemporary Christians* (Minneapolis: Fortress Press, 1990).

14. *Ibid.*, pp. 57-58.

15. Barbara Brown Taylor, *The Preaching Life* (Cambridge: Cowley Publications, 1993), p. 81.

16. Luke Timothy Johnson, *The Writings of the New Testament* (Philadelphia: Fortress Press, 1986), p. 548. My views on canon are obviously indebted to Johnson and to Brevard S. Childs, *Introduction to the Old Testament as Scripture* (Philadelphia: Fortress Press, 1979), and *The New Testament as Canon: An Introduction* (Philadelphia: Fortress Press, 1984).

17. Johnson, *Faith's Freedom*, p. 76.

18. William Placher, "The Nature of Biblical Authority: Issues and Models from Recent Theology," in *Conservative, Moderate, Liberal: The Biblical Authority Debate*, ed. Charles R. Blaisdell, papers presented at a conference held at Christian Theological Seminary, Sept. 27-28, 1989 (St. Louis: CBP Press, 1990), p. 5.

Chapter 4

Reading To The Congregation

For about a year I attended a church whose preacher had a peculiar obsession. In every sermon he included a mini-lesson about biblical studies; one Greek, Latin, Hebrew, or German technical term was used and explained each week. Once we heard an explication (slightly inaccurate) of the form-critical expression *Sitz im Leben*. Another time we were treated to a whole sermon on the Hebrew word for "righteousness," every other sentence beginning with the word *sedaqah*. The odd thing was how haphazard these references to scholarship were; they often seemed to be stuck in as afterthoughts — "Paul speaks of the 'mystery,' which reminds me that there were these things called 'mystery religions' ... but that's not relevant to what Paul is saying." I speculated that, in his annual review, a church member must have told him that "we want more Bible teaching from the pulpit" and this was his answer. Later I described these sermons to a friend who, it turned out, had started going to that same church after I left. "Really?" my friend said. "Our preacher rarely mentions biblical studies and never uses technical terms in the pulpit." I surmised that someone must have told him to stop.

I find that when I speak of the sermon as "reading the biblical text," hands fly up in objection. "Their eyes glaze over," experienced preachers complain, "when we talk about Jesus, let alone mention Bultmann." Many preachers, faced with the prospect of an entire glazed-over congregation, are tempted to skip the biblical stuff and get on to rhetoric. Here is where imagination, wit, lucidity, eloquence — all the outward characteristics we usually associate with a good preacher — have their place. This is what the preacher is usually praised for and, vanity aside, the words of the Sunday sermon take on a central role for both preacher and community. The sermon is the pastor's most public offering and in many churches serves as the centerpiece of the Sunday service. "Surely," my objectors will say, "we must give the congregation something that holds their interest — and it's not to be found on a dusty library shelf."

The objectors are usually surprised when I agree with them. Nothing could be duller than a sermon about Bultmann, and even Jesus can be dehydrated, shriveled to a desiccated crust. It all depends on how we preachers make use of the work we have done on biblical texts. We cannot cut and paste our study notes into the sermon, technical terms and all. We must be more discriminating. Many have found, however, that their theological training majored in the reading of texts, but only minored in the art of eloquence, perhaps even leaving it to independent study. The thing the preacher is best rewarded for — being interesting in the pulpit — was often learned there by sheer trial and error.

Preachers will do well to take to heart a distinction made by Fred Craddock: the process of coming to have something to say is different from the process of saying it.[1] Study and composition are distinct endeavors. To rephrase in the terms I have used in this book, when one moves from studying the text to composing the sermon, one changes interpretive communities. In studying the biblical text, the preacher sits not only with the congregation but also among the guild of biblical scholars, and alongside the interpretation of the church over the years. When one stands in the pulpit, however, the audience has shifted. Here are people who do not know Bultmann or any of his kin. They come to listen, but most come cold. They have not studied this week's text and have probably not even read it, being preoccupied with other things — their jobs, their families, their hobbies, the latest community issue or news flash. Even the preacher who leads the congregation in formal Bible studies during the week must take into account that not all participated, and that there may always be that one stranger who walked in off the street. The process of coming to have something to say in the pulpit must be different from actually saying it, because the audience of one preacher sitting before the biblical text has given way to a congregation of many.

The preacher must observe this distinction between study and composition, between content and form. Preachers who take this simple contrast to heart will be much clearer about the preaching task, and their sermons will improve exponentially. While study and composition are related, they are not identical. Certainly at times the preacher looks up from a Raymond Brown tome with a glimmer in the eye, and the sermon suddenly takes shape. These moments of grace cannot be ignored but must not be taken for granted. Usually, however, study does not yield a sermon *per se*. The study process brings to the preacher a message from the outside and thus adds depth and breadth to the sermon, giving the preacher something to say that was learned and not already known. No one can avoid the hard process of studying the text week after week without falling into the shallow end of the pool. Still, that hard process is only half the work.

The preacher begins in the study, but at a certain point must move toward the pulpit. How does one know when it's time to move from study to composition, and how does one make that move? I recommend that the preacher stay with study until something has been learned — some sense of otherness is at hand. (To restate this principle negatively, the preacher who picks up the next commentary and finds nothing new may move on). When the preacher has dug deeply into the biblical text and found there a trace of otherness, it is time to head back to the present.

There are various ways to move from study to composition. The preacher may conclude study by summarizing both content and form of the biblical lection, answering in simple sentences the questions, "What does the text say?" and "What does the text do?" The preacher similarly may write yet another sentence: a single positive statement of the sermon's theme as the first step in composition. (The preacher who writes such sentences must certainly have read Craddock's textbook, *Preaching*, since this is exactly what Craddock advises.) In addition to such sentence-writing, the preacher may, between biblical study and the composition of the sermon, engage in other exercises to stimulate the imagination: doodling on scratch paper, listing personal or parish concerns, brainstorming possible sermon angles, doing free-association on words and phrases drawn from the lections. Mind you, we have not yet begun the composition process — what comes out on paper here may make it into the sermon but is often too undisciplined. The movement between study and composition may not involve pen and paper at all and may not take place consciously: the preacher may read the newspaper, flip through magazines or favorite books, go for a walk, play tennis, or meditate. Each one of us has different ways to get the creative juices flowing. Much more could be said about the step between the study and the pulpit, but I do not need to duplicate what can be found in any textbook.[2]

The composition process itself is, like the study process before it, improved with practice and training. Sermon composition is something that can be developed and refined. This statement goes against the grain of what is commonly believed. Indeed, the public talents of the preacher are often underestimated by congregations because they seem to be natural rather than learned skills. "We're so lucky," the congregation says, "to have a natural-born speaker." In fact, I have often been told, when I have announced that I teach preaching, that no such thing can possibly be taught. But like the skills of exegesis, the skills of rhetoric are learned behaviors. The preacher must become skilled at both, even if only one set of skills shows. The truth is that without highly-developed and practiced skill in the composition and delivery of a sermon, whatever interpretive brilliance the preacher may have displayed in the study will go unnoticed.

Again, the standard textbooks provide general guidance on the composition of the sermon, and I will not rehash that advice here. My main concern in this chapter is to examine the implications for sermon composition of what I have written so far in this book. I have argued that the preacher studies within more than one interpretive community but preaches to a much more limited audience; the sermon is to create for that second group a new world in light of whatever glimpse of Otherness the preacher has caught during the study process. What will this mean as the sermon spins itself out? I believe that the sermon's form springs from much the same reading processes that are at work in the preacher's study. The preacher reads a text in order to create a text. The created text is the sermon, which is itself a reading of the biblical text. The preacher produces a new text in, with, and for the congregation. All the same dynamics of reading at work in the study will be at work in the pulpit.

Please note that when I speak of the sermon being a "text" or a "reading," I am not implying anything about what manuscript or notes the preacher takes into the pulpit (more on this subject later). I speak of "reading" to a congregation in the broadest sense: the act of interpretation. "Reading" consists of the processes of study, composition, and communication, the ways of putting what one has learned into a presentable form. The "text" of the sermon is what happens on Sunday morning.

The text of the sermon arises from two related aspects. First, the sermon is an oral text. No matter what writing has gone into the processes of study and composition, the ultimate product is speech. Second, as with any text, there will be gaps in the sermon for the readers (listeners) to fill in. The preacher who has examined all the implications of these two aspects of the sermonic text will know a great deal about how to compose an effective sermon. Formal structures and the language of the sermon follow from its basic oral nature and the way hearers fill in its gaps. Once one has understood orality, gaps, and their interplay, all else follows.

Orality: The Text In Time

The form and language of the sermon follows first of all from its most basic characteristic: it is an oral presentation. It takes place in a certain space and time. It is a bodily presentation; that is, the speaker is present with the audience. While there is inevitably nonverbal, visual, bodily communication, the primary emphasis is on the spoken word.[3] The text of the sermon is oral. Even when read straight off the pages of a manuscript, the sermon is oral. No listener can go back and reread the last sentence. A poorly constructed sentence, one that is unclear or ambiguous, cannot be properly attended to by the listeners; if they stop to figure it out, they miss the next part of the text. If their minds stray ever so briefly, yet another sentence or two is dropped. It is easy to see that a few bad sentences and a couple of irrelevant thoughts can put the message into serious jeopardy. The preacher has a job tougher than that of putting words physically on a page; the words must be put into ears, and in such a way that the mind will not stray. Orality is the most basic truth to be grasped about the text of the sermon, with profound implications for its composition. The need for orality implies certain kinds of language and structures and excludes others.

Take, for example, a simple transition from one idea to another. Suppose, in a sermon on the parable of the sower, I want to move the congregation from a common interpretation to a more unusual position — from seeing themselves as the various types of soils to seeing the sower as the God who sows with gracious abandon. I write,

> *I know a lot of people who read this story and start worrying. "What kind of soil am I?" they say. "Am I really worthy?" "Shouldn't I be doing more to prove that God has really sown the gospel in me?" I've always believed that if you weren't good soil, you probably wouldn't be here in church. And you certainly wouldn't be listening to me.*
>
> *And besides, maybe your soil type is not the point.*

With the last sentence, my focus has begun to change. If I were writing, I could use a visual, typographical device to signify a change of subject. The most conventional is the paragraph, which is what I have used above; the text is indented so many spaces in order to signify the change. Verbal clues may be added: "It follows that ..." "Another way of looking at this is ..."; here I have used, "And besides...." Most importantly, as a writer I may count on you the reader to read until understanding occurs. I may write a transition sentence that is tightly packed, hoping that the one who looks at my words will be inclined to take the time to stare until they yield meaning.

In a sermon, however, I cannot rely on any of this. Visual clues are offered not by a written page but by the actual physical presence of the author. Paragraphing is out; when I speak the lines above, you cannot see the indentation of my paragraphs.[4] Such verbal clues as I have used are helpful, and I may also vary my posture or change my delivery style. But these alone will not make an effective transition. Ultimately I must rely on words.

The transition in the sermon is very tricky indeed; it must get words to do its work. In order to change gears and move from one subject to another, the hearers need what only the author can grant, time — time to close off one set of thoughts, time to adjust to a new thought, time for the mind to wander a bit before it recenters itself in a new place. Time in an oral presentation is dictated by the author, not the reader. Only the preacher, through the construction of the sermon, can give the listeners this time. A pause may be helpful (and there is probably too little silence in today's sermons), but spoken words can also be arranged in ways that give the listeners time to listen. The preacher can offer a kind of controlled verbosity that would be horribly redundant in written work, but is just right in making an oral transition. David Buttrick has argued that any transition in a sermon must take at least three sentences.[5] If I follow Buttrick's suggestion, I may go on with the transition as follows:

> *And besides, maybe your soil type is not the point. Maybe we don't have to think of ourselves as the soil in this parable. Maybe we should have a different focus. Let's think not about the soil, but about the sower.*

One may debate the three-sentence rule (though I tend to think it a good one), but the point stands: to make a transition of subjects, the preacher must offer the people some time to fix the new subject firmly in mind.

The sermon is a text, but it is not written. Composing a sermon differs markedly from a routine written assignment, because the sermon will ultimately be spoken. Note that I speak of "composing" a sermon, not "writing" one, because I hope this language will transform the way preachers think about the process of composition. The sermon can at no time be reduced to a series of words on a page, and in the end it bears little relation to whatever written delivery aids the preacher may use. It is best to realize this from the beginning so that the sermon's orality sits before the preacher always. One who writes a manuscript does better to write with the ear in mind from the start and perhaps does best to speak the words aloud as they are written. The end process of sermon composition is never a written text. The sermon is not a written creation prepared for oral delivery. The sermon is the oral delivery itself.

I must also note at this point that when I speak of the sermon as an oral presentation, I imply nothing about the preacher's mode of composition or delivery, only the final product. That is to say, I am not making another statement in the tired old "Manuscript vs. Notes" war. Good sermons are produced with manuscripts, without manuscripts, with notes, and without notes — in any and every way imaginable. The real question, I think, is how the preacher best utilizes writing to produce the ultimate product.[6] Most great lines in great speeches were put on a page before they were spoken: "Four score and seven years ago ..." "We have nothing to fear but fear itself ..." "Ask not what your country can do for you...." All these lines were written, but they were written to be spoken, and that makes all the difference. There is no question that great oral words can be written down, but every political speechwriter knows that writing for the TelePrompTer is different from writing for the op-ed page. On the other hand, many fine sermons are carefully composed and preached without a scrap of paper; some preachers actually do worse when forced to write things down. "Oral" does not mean an unrelated series of unprepared digressions.

True, most preachers probably need the discipline of a written manuscript in order to focus their thoughts and language, and many want the comfort of having that manuscript before them in the pulpit. Each preacher will want to determine for him/herself how best to compose the sermon and what to use in the pulpit. Though I personally rarely take a manuscript into the pulpit now, I spent seven years preaching with a manuscript before me. Usually I write every word of my sermon down verbatim before I preach; other times I compose certain parts (often stories) orally just before Sunday morning, going over it again and again until it's ready. Sometimes the right words for a certain section don't come until I stand before the congregation, and I am surprised to find that what came out of my mouth was exactly what I meant, but didn't know how, to say. The goal of sermon composition is not the writing but the speaking, the hearing not the seeing; the written creation, if it exists at all, is the servant of the main, oral event. The sermon is not finished with the production or even the revision of a manuscript. The sermon is not finished until it is preached.

Gaps: Holes In The Sermon

With an oral text as with any text, there are gaps to be filled in by the readers. "Gaps," you will recall from Chapter 2, are empty spots in a text which a reader (hearer) must fill in with the necessary literary, social, cultural, psychological, historical, or other kind of information in order to understand that text fully. Gaps are what the hearer of a sermon supplies to make sense of the whole. Not everything is said, no matter how plain the speaker. This is not a failing in a sermon; in fact, it makes communication possible. Communication engages, it is not merely passive. A reader must work to interpret a text. Were it not so, our daily conversations and routine communications would be dull and tedious indeed. A text with no gaps would take on the features of a "Conehead" sketch from *Saturday Night Live*: "Use your upper right appendage to grasp the implement intended for the application of soft dairy products to baked grain consumables and extend it toward my upper left appendage" would be ordinary conversation were it not for our ability to fill in gaps. How much easier to say, "Pass the butter knife."

So too the sermon takes into account the listeners of the sermon — as "readers" they need work to do. It is important for the preacher to provide an appropriately-gapped text. On the one hand, not everything can be spelled out, lest one bore the listener with the predictable and the telegraphed. Nothing so spoils a sermon as belaboring the obvious. For example, does every proverb or cliché need to be quoted in its entirety, especially when the preacher intends to acknowledge its proverbial or clichéd nature? Why not leave it open-ended: "You know what they say, 'A bird in the hand...' "? Many preachers expound on the moral of a story that was completely obvious to everyone who heard it, or treat a contemporary news event as if no one read the newspaper or watched *Nightline*. For events and people well-grounded in the public consciousness, a passing allusion will go much further than a lengthy and unnecessary explanation. It may be appropriate to tell the story of Jimmy Stewart's George Bailey in *It's a Wonderful Life*, but it is a crime to tell it as if the movie did not play a thousand times on television that December.

On the other hand, the preacher must be careful not to assume too much. One cannot offer chasms and expect hearers to bridge them. An allusion to Edward R. Murrow will be greeted with stony stares by a roomful of teenagers, unless they are attending a "History of Journalism" class. Bart Simpson will command greater recognition from the teenagers, though perhaps not from their grandparents. A great deal depends on the kind of gap-filling the preacher expects a congregation to do. One can no longer assume, as in the past, extensive knowledge of the Bible or Shakespeare. It can be dangerous to make the most elementary assumptions about a congregation. The preacher cannot assume, for example, that all the hearers went to college, or attended Sunday school, or loved their parents — these kinds of assumptions may affect the preacher's credibility and can make or break the sermon. The distinction between an effective gap and a yawning chasm is sometimes slim; I have found, experimenting with my preaching classes, that if I say, "He was like Bart Simpson," many students will protest that they've never watched the show, but if I say, "He had a haircut like Bart Simpson's," nearly everyone smiles and laughs. The jagged head of Bart Simpson, at least, is a cultural phenomenon.

It is impossible to communicate without making assumptions about the audience, but the making of assumptions is fraught with peril. The preacher finds herself in a Catch-22. Fortunately, the process of gap-making and gap-filling is so instinctive to the communication process that we get much of it right without trying. Still, it is a good exercise every now and again for the preacher to go over a sermon and ask what kind of gaps are built into it, and what kind of listener is implied by those gaps. The preacher who leaves too few and too elementary gaps insults the hearers, as does the preacher who leaves too many and too difficult.

Attention to gaps will mean attention to sermon form. Different literary forms offer different kinds of gaps, some of which are useful in an oral text such as a sermon. A familiar hymn may provide an adequate homiletic climax, but a complex poem meant to be read with the eyes as well as the ears will not. Jesus used parables and proverbs in his preaching, but not riddles, and for good reason. A parable requires more thinking than a proverb, but a riddle may require so much thinking as to be inappropriate in an oral presentation. The hearers need work to do but not puzzles to sort out; there is simply not enough time to stop and solve the puzzle, as the sermon and the liturgy must move on. Unfortunately, many contemporary preachers, thinking they are using "inductive" or "narrative" methods, offer riddles to their congregations, juxtaposing images and stories without transition or comment. There is a difference between letting the hearers think for themselves and simply being obscure.

Nevertheless, all sermons have gaps, and often the most interesting sermons have the most interesting gaps. The preacher takes a risk when composing a sermon: here one is offering the listeners a gap and hopes that they will be able to fill it in. The preacher may or may not hit the mark, and it may or may not make a difference in how the listeners hear the sermon. For example, my sermon may contain these lines:

> *There are some people, they call themselves social reformers, but what's their program, what's their reform? They seem more interested in destruction: let's tear down the system, toss the rich into exile. They don't like the powers that be, but the power they want is no better. They just want to bring the walls down. Haven't we had enough of that brand of reform in the last few centuries, in the years between Madame Defarge and Pol Pot?*

I close with a fairly complex allusion, and I take a risk: my professionally-educated congregation may or may not remember Madame Defarge from their grade-school reading of Dickens' *A Tale of Two Cities*, and despite the acclaimed film *The Killing Fields*, they are even less likely to recognize the name of the deposed Cambodian despot who filled those fields with blood. On the other hand, this congregation did go to grade school, does read and does watch movies. Further, if I have made my point well up to this line,

I will have offered my hearers information enough to fill the gaps adequately if not completely — whether the names seem vaguely familiar or entirely alien, it is clear that these two persons committed dastardly acts in the name of social reform. I decide to let the allusion stand, because it makes the section more interesting, and I am convinced that most people will get it. However, I may be wrong, so I will be careful in the rest of my sermon, knowing that hearers are forgiving of one or two overwide gaps but not a whole string of them. As time goes on, I will be able to target my gaps more carefully, especially if I have established ways to gather honest feedback.

Form

Studies of the sermon sometimes seem to concentrate almost exclusively on the way the sermon is framed, what homileticians generally refer to as the sermon's structure or "form." The latest bestseller in homiletics often proves to be an essay on form, extolling the virtues of this or that form for communicating to the weary masses. Congregations whose preachers read these books are treated to a succession of inductive sermons, then a series of narrative sermons, then a rash of phenomenological sermons, and so it goes, on and on. If the pastorate is long enough, parishioners may be able to spot the trends.

By contrast, other preachers pay scant attention to form, preferring to work by intuition. They do not sit down and say, "I will compose my message using such-and-such a form." They simply compose. Textbooks which advocate a certain form seem irrelevant to these preachers. Why bother worrying about something that is, after all, like the paper sack that carries your groceries from the store? We're cooking a meal here.

I find myself somewhere between these two extremes. While I do not wish the preacher to neglect form, I do not intend to advocate a certain form as *the* form of the sermon. "Sermon" is not in and of itself a genre but encompasses many different forms. The form of the sermon has varied widely over the years. The modern narrative sermon bears little resemblance to the biblical expositions of Augustine. The patristic Greek homily was quite different from the sermonette which some today, in the mistaken impression that the "-ly" is a diminutive, call a "homily." The medieval university sermon is certainly the predecessor of what is now known as "the traditional three-point sermon," but the complex rules for composing the older variety have long since disappeared. Again, I will leave the complete listing of possible forms to the textbooks.[7] Suffice it to say that what passes for a "sermon" can vary widely from time to time, from place to place, and even, as we have seen, from one church to another in the same town. Though some homileticians would have it otherwise, there is no one form we can point to and say, "This is the sermon."

Variety in sermonic form is not a bad thing; in fact, I would like to hear such variation even from a single pulpit. Diversity in form helps keep both preacher and congregation on their toes; this week's sermon will not be predictable because it is palpably different from last week's. The preacher who takes seriously the task of interpreting biblical passages will automatically vary the forms because some forms lend themselves to a certain passage while others do not. One best not preach a parable as an argument, or a doxology as a command; to do so is to treat the biblical text capriciously and thus to diminish its authority. Further, form and content, though not identical, are related. Thus the preacher who uses only one form may seem to be saying the same thing over and over again, no matter how the actual content of the sermon changes. Since the world of the congregation is formed over many sermons, the congregation who hears one and only one kind of sermon may grow lopsided, if at all.

Thus preachers should pay attention to form and not leave it entirely to intuition. One may be composing in the same form time and again without realizing it; it would be a helpful exercise for preachers to review the forms of several recent sermons. It may well be that one's supposedly intuitive sermon form actually follows a routine pattern week after week. If awareness of form causes the preacher to vary the pattern even a little bit, the congregation will sit up to listen.

More than that, the preacher must realize that form implies content, and vice versa. Those who denigrate form do not realize the close relation between form and content. Form is more than a paper sack to carry the goods in; form is a part of the meaning. A doxology is supposed to produce wonder; it cannot carry an argument. A traditional riddle brings puzzlement, then clarity, while a Zen Buddhist koan may do the opposite. A parable is meant to be pondered, a command to be accepted. One cannot separate the content from these forms; meaning is inherent in them. The preacher who wishes to communicate effectively must use the proper tools. What is best conveyed by telling a series of stories will find three points and a poem a poor medium.

Awareness of form during composition can also help the preacher target the message. A message which says, "It's either this or that," requires a clear "Either/Or" form, while a message which says "It may be this, or it may be that," needs "Both/And," not "Either/Or." Many writers have had the experience that only when nascent ideas are put on paper and take on a structure do their deeper meanings bubble up to the surface. Attention to form may help clarify the preacher's true meaning and thus produce better preaching.

Orality, Gaps, And Form

While I do not advocate one particular form over another, I do believe that all sermonic forms share some general features. All sermon forms must be suitable for oral delivery. Sermons have to be spoken aloud within the allotted time and must be grasped by the hearer within the speaker's time frame. Certain forms do not lend themselves to preaching; neither the riddle, the theological treatise, nor the novel will do. Further, any sermonic form must be appropriately gapped for the listeners; the gaps must be present, interesting, and manageable. The gaps follow from the oral nature of the sermon.

As we have already seen, a sermon is an oral presentation and moves in time. It is time-bound, using so many minutes, no less, no more. This has implications for the sermon's form. The features of a good oral form are to some extent the features of time itself. For one thing, time moves forward and never backward, Einstein and science fiction notwithstanding. Until we humans learn a way to maneuver in space warps at the speed of light, we are consigned to forward, linear existence. The sermon likewise must move forward and take its listeners with it. They cannot go back and reread the beginning, nor will they lounge around the opening sentences for long, lest the message leave the station without them. The sermon must move, and it must move forward.

Here lies one problem with sermon composition as it is generally perceived. Beginning students of preaching are usually taught to sum up their sermon in one sentence that will contain the distillation of the entire message. This procedure is well and good and, in fact, essential if one's sermon is to be a unified whole. The question is what one does with such a sentence, now that the time has come to compose a sermon. One of the legacies of this so-called "distillation method" of preaching is that it produces many sermons with little movement. This happens when the preacher puts the sermon sentence up front and then elaborates on it with illustrative material. The result is a sermon that is curiously flat and stationary, like a joke which goes on and on after the punchline. The point has been made early on, and what remains are stories intended to be amusing or heart-rending that nevertheless fall flat and seem anti-climatic.

The mistake here is to put the conclusion in the introduction. The sermon theme sentence, if it is to appear in the sermon and not be merely a compositional aid, must go somewhere near the end of the sermon — it is the goal of the message, not the starting point. Craddock speaks of the quality of "anticipation," and I have heard him use the example of a grandfather who slowly peels an apple for his young grandson, laboriously turning the fruit a tiny bit at a time under the pocketknife, carefully keeping the red skin intact in one long sliver, until the smells and the juices and the grandfather's slow movements produce a burst of apple-lust in the young child. Anticipation requires two things: the sermon must have a goal and, like the grandfather, it must exercise restraint in getting there.[8] In the language of this book, the sermon must contain appropriate gaps. The preacher cannot give everything away in the first five minutes. But after fifteen minutes, there should have been a payoff. The congregation that is not prepared for eating by sight, sound, and smell will not take the apple from the hand of the preacher, but woe to the preacher who offers sight, sound, and smell, but no apple in the end.

The preacher must beware, however, of offering false suspense in place of true anticipation. Movement that has a trivial goal irritates listeners more than no movement at all; the people have trusted the preacher to go so far, but in the end they are disappointed to be offered nothing so substantive as an apple. The recent homiletical emphasis on storytelling has perhaps encouraged preachers into too much description and too many plot twists, so that a simple example about, say, being stuck in an elevator becomes a five minute story which covers every step towards the elevator. Again, the preacher must consider the time of the listeners; if you spend one third of the sermon getting there, the payoff better be big or the disappointment will be great. Unless every step to that elevator is crucial, the story had best begin, "I was stuck in an elevator once." Think of the movement of the sermon as a whole, as well as the movement of a particular section. Seen in light of the whole sermon, the elevator story will probably prove to be a step elsewhere, not a stopping place of its own.

False anticipation becomes particularly problematic when preachers use what I call the "Garrison Keillor opening," after the radio performer who traipses all around Lake Wobegon until he finally gets to the main story of the night. What works for Keillor on the radio rarely works in the pulpit, in part because few of us are Garrison Keillor, but mainly because we are preaching and not just telling stories. We are trying to move toward a message and cannot afford to give the congregation so many places to jump off. Suppose the sermon opens,

> The night I graduated from college, we had a whopper of an all-night party. I woke up at noon with a pounding head and realized that I had less than 24 hours to be at my new job in Dallas. I hopped into my decrepit '64 Thunderbird and drove and drove and drove, through Georgia, Alabama, Mississippi. When I reached Louisi-

ana, a sign flashed in my headlights. The sign said....

The preacher no doubt wishes to make a point about what the sign said, and that point may well be a worthy starting point for the sermon. But if the congregation is a little tired and confused by the time they get to the sign, who can blame them? They have finished college, experienced a hangover, waxed nostalgic over their first car, and traveled through four states, only to find all these things mere distractions from their goal. If the preacher wants an awake and alert congregation to read the sign, all this prelude should be skipped. When our story stops at five places before it arrives at its point, we simply give people five other things to think about.

Sermon forms come in many flavors, and all are worth sampling. No matter what form the sermon takes, it must move forward and take the congregation with it. The skilled preacher builds in gaps in such a way that the listeners' minds are kept busy the whole way. Too many or too obscure gaps, and their minds shut down from too much stimulation. Too few or too obvious gaps, and their minds go to sleep long before the end. The preacher will do well to set for each sermon a worthy goal and then to consider the appropriate length for each step in the journey toward that goal.

The Bible And Form

Fortunately the challenge of creating and using appropriate oral forms is aided by the preacher's subject matter. Much of the Bible, particularly the New Testament, was composed for oral presentation.[9] Reading in the ancient world was less a private, visual event than it is now. There were no printing presses. People usually read aloud even when reading privately, and not everyone was fluent in reading and writing. If one had need of a written document, scribes were widely available for hire in the Greek or Roman marketplace. Those who were trained to read and write were trained under the rules of classical rhetoric and wrote according to the rules of oral presentation. The letters of Paul and his disciples were read aloud in the churches to which they were addressed (cf. Colossians 4:16, "And when this letter has been read among you, have it read also in the church of the Laodiceans"). Thus the words of the New Testament were more likely to be heard than seen. Many rhetorical skills can be learned by the preacher who studies the forms of the Bible. Jesus was a master storyteller, Paul a great debater. Forms taken from the Bible are by their very nature amenable to the spoken word. Again, textbooks will provide numerous examples.[10]

Taking one's form from the Bible is no guarantee of effective communication, of course. I remember vividly a student sermon on 2 Peter 1:16, "For we did not follow cleverly devised myths when we made known to you the power and coming of our Lord Jesus Christ, but we had been eyewitnesses of his majesty." The first half of the sermon was a dreadfully dull rehash of certain dubious scholarly theories about the composition of 2 Peter; this section had little movement and no apparent point. The second half, however, was glorious: it was a colorful, dynamic account of the faith of the preacher's grandfather, an old Greek fisherman. In discussion afterwards, the class didn't quite know what to make of it until we turned our attention to the form of sermon. We realized that the form was "Not this/But this," taken right from the biblical lection: "Not cleverly devised myths/But eyewitnesses to his majesty." The student preacher had learned her lesson too well and nearly killed the sermon with her deadly recounting of "cleverly devised myths."

Wherever we find our forms, we must realize that form as structure is a frame, a means to an end, not the point itself. True, form and content are close relatives. But form works for content, and not vice versa. The form that calls attention to itself is a poor form; if the studs are showing, the walls are thin indeed. A typical congregation will never know what kind of form the preacher is using, nor need they. Even a trained critical listener may not be able to recognize a complex form. One student preached in class on the Prodigal Son and was quite indignant when no one in the class realized that his sermon form matched the story point for point. I had to explain that people cannot get their ears around that kind of complexity, even when they are explicitly listening for form. Our congregations, not training to be preachers themselves, will be busy at work in the routine gap-filling that an oral text requires. Form provides certain kinds of gaps but is not itself a gap that listeners must fill. Attention to form is, like the critical study of a biblical text, an invisible but necessary job; the preacher can afford neither to neglect it nor to let it show. There are no awards in preaching for great form, though the preacher and the congregation will reap rewards in clarity, variety, and interest.

Language

Language, too, is one of the formal characteristics of a sermon. My distinction between the sermon's form and its language is somewhat artificial, as is the distinction between form and content — whether viewed as form or content, the sermon is made up of words. It is worthwhile, however, for the preacher to consider what kind of words go into a sermon. If it is to be an effective oral presentation, those words must work well orally. The preacher, unlike most authors, composes for the ear, not the eye. There is an oral language that differs from the standard written word, and the preacher must become a master of this language. The message is too important to neglect the words that convey it.

Language is not the whole sermon, but it is hard to imagine, apart from experiments in mime or liturgical dance, a sermon without language, and even harder to imagine a good sermon without good language. True, preaching is in some quarters considered merely a branch of public speaking, and some homileticians seem to make language the main point of their work. I do not believe that preaching can be reduced to mere rhetoric and verbal display, but I sympathize with those who labor to reform the language of the pulpit. While it is lamentable that the complex tasks involved in preaching are sometimes reduced to mere speechwriting, it is more disheartening to hear preachers speak in jargon and clichés. If everything happening in the church is, according to the preacher, "wonderful" or "marvelous," what words can we use to account for the mundane, and what language can express the exceptional? How can the preacher "share his feelings" with us unless we are empaths? How many times must the congregation listen to sentences that begin, "We live in a society that ..." "When I read this morning's lesson, I felt ..." or "The good news is ..."? Like form, language is a tool. It is not the message, but it cannot be neglected without great peril to the message.

The preacher's language will improve only with careful attention. The pulpit suffers if the preacher's study contains only commentaries and Bible dictionaries. It is essential that the preacher also study how to communicate. The advice routinely given to budding authors applies as well to preachers: if one would write, one must read. We preachers will be enriched by reading the great communicators in many fields — the best journalists, science writers, essayists, poets, and fiction writers. A short story a week is a good discipline (one I often assign to classes), not just for stimulating language skills but also to see how a subject can be handled in short scope. Certainly one can benefit from reading the publications of other preachers. But any study of written language stops just short of the crucial need of the preacher: to learn how to speak.

Orality, Gaps, And Language

The language of the sermon is oral language. Here the preacher must depart from written models and forge into new territory. This is difficult for some; our educational system has rewarded us for reading with our lips closed while sitting quietly at our desks. So part of the preacher's continuing education may be to eavesdrop on conversations or to pay close attention to radio and television announcers. Speaking is not the same thing as writing and, given our formal training in writing, we often lapse into old written habits when composing a sermon. When the congregation complains that the sermon doesn't sound like the preacher is really talking to them, they are probably picking up on such written style as has stolen into the sermon manuscript. The characteristics of written style are easily catalogued: the brief, compact expressions, the complex sentences, the tendency to abstraction. Add the awkward, unvarying pace that often accompanies the reading of a manuscript, and you have all the marks of a sermon that looks better than it sounds.

One helpful solution to this problem I have already mentioned: speak aloud as you compose. If the sermon is to be written out word-for-word, each word can be spoken as it is written. If the preacher works from a sketch or outline, the main sections, transitions, and other important passages can be verbalized from the start. This discipline will remove much of the awkwardness from the final product. Written-sounding language will also be difficult to read aloud; if it's hard to say, it will be hard to hear and must be changed. Composing orally from the beginning can save the preacher many drafts in the end.

The preacher will also be aided by learning some of the basic features of spoken, as opposed to written, language. If one writes out a sermon manuscript, one can learn to write for oral presentation, using an oral style. Again, mastering the peculiarities of oral style can save the preacher much preparation time.

Oral language, for example, must be fairly simple in construction. Complex, lengthy sentences are not particularly easy to hear, especially sentences in which the hearer must suspend, say, a subject, while the verb waits for the rest of the sentence to finish. To take a hypothetical example, suppose a sermon on 2 Corinthians contains the following section:

> *Paul, who had been worried about the Corinthian church, and had sent Titus to deliver his most recent letter, and had found his prolonged absence upsetting, since he did not know how his instructions had been received, now rejoiced in his coming.*

As it stands, this passage is in severe need of revision. The long wait between the subject "Paul" and the verb "rejoiced" makes this sentence particularly difficult to hear. It would be better recast into a series of shorter sentences:

> *Paul was worried about the Corinthian church and had sent Titus to deliver his most recent letter. He had found his prolonged absence upsetting, since he did not know how his instructions had been received. But now he rejoiced in his coming.*

Though it is better, this section is not yet suited to oral delivery.

For one thing, it has several loosely-connected pronouns. The preacher must remember that a hearer cannot look back to see who "he" or "his" referred to. Here is where the gaps of an oral text differ from the gaps of a written text. Written texts can make great use of shortcuts, such as pronouns. Oral texts must be much more careful to make their meaning clear. A "this" or "that" that works fine on the written page is often best replaced by its actual referent. In the example above, our preacher might revise as follows (note that some of the sentence structures are changed to avoid monotony):

> *Paul was worried about the Corinthian church and had sent Titus to deliver his most recent letter. He had found Titus' prolonged absence upsetting; after all, Paul did not know how his instructions had been received. But now he rejoiced in the coming of Titus.*

The unclear referent is a particular problem for preachers, as it often introduces a gap the congregation finds impossible to fill. The preacher should routinely check for this kind of gap in a text, which can occur with verbs and nouns as well as pronouns. For example, suppose a sermon on Philippians closes thus:

> *Even in jail, Paul can say, "I rejoice in the Lord greatly." This is no show. He really does rejoice. Bound, gagged and chained, Paul can rejoice. Maybe I can, too.*

The gap here is that the hearer must supply the final verb. Since this is the closing line, and "rejoice" is the crucial word in this ending, it is probably best to close this gap for the hearer and revise to "Maybe I can rejoice, too." This has the advantage of giving the preacher an emphatic word in the final sentence, and also offers relief to any listener who strayed just before the last line (" 'Maybe I can, too'? Maybe I can what?").

In short, the gaps are different in oral presentations than in typical written language. Sentences must be shorter and clearer and must account for the occasional wandering of mind. Meaning must be readily apparent on the first hearing. That which is unintentionally ambiguous to the ear must go. Give the people something to think about, but never leave them puzzling over a bad sentence. There are enough gaps in life without having to fill in those left by a vague, inaccurate, or careless speaker.

Language Concrete And Vivid

Oral composition differs from written not only in sentence construction, but also in the vocabulary used. Oral composition requires a preference for concrete rather than abstract words for two reasons. One is the element of time; readers of written texts can take their time in dealing with abstract concepts, while hearers of time-bound oral presentations cannot. Secondly, concrete language makes up for what the oral presentation lacks, a visual component. A reader has a visual aid, the words on a page. Apart from body language, the only visual aid the speaker can evoke is the imagination of the hearer.

The truth is that words that evoke sight, sound, and touch are easier to hear (as well as easier to say). The preacher will do well to use words that produce a picture or a sensation, words that one can touch or smell or feel. The "family pet" evokes no image, or maybe too many, where "short-haired tabby" presents a clear picture. Abstractions such as "relationships" should not crowd real-life husbands, wives, lovers, mothers, fathers, sons, daughters, and friends from our sermons. Some preachers labor under the misapprehension that they must use general language so that everyone will relate, but the opposite is true: people relate to the specific. No one admits to having "stressful relationships," but if the preacher says, "The husband is out of town again, dinner is late, and the kids are banging on the pots and pans," then a lot of women in the pews will be nodding their heads.

Hand in hand with concrete nouns go vivid verbs. Must everyone "walk" down the street, or do some "skip," "float," "stride," "flutter," "sail," "slide," "roll," or "putter"? Fill in the verb in the sentence, "She ____ a tender farewell." It's amazing how many different verbs will fit there, and what a wide range of meaning is created with each new verb, from "waved," "whispered," and "choked," to "barked," "bluffed," and even "spat." One need not dip deeply into the thesaurus to find expressive verbs; all these examples are part of normal, everyday speech.

The preacher will do well to rely on verbs and nouns rather than adverbs or adjectives, which weaken and clutter the sermon. The dull sentence "I lay on the green grass" is improved simply by omitting "green"; one assumes grass is green, especially since people do not usually lie on the grass in the winter. If more is needed, the sentence can be further improved by the addition of a more evocative verb: "I lounged on the grass." Again, study of the great communicators will show the way; literature is written mainly with nouns and verbs, with adjectives and adverbs added only when needed. Here good written and oral styles coincide. Strong, vivid verbs and concrete nouns are the backbone of the sermon. While the use of slang can make a sermon sound too cute or trendy, the preacher will not go wrong using "slang" as defined by the poet Carl Sandburg: "A language that rolls up its sleeves, spits on its hands, and goes to work." (Here is an example of language that does what it says!)

To return to our revision of the paragraph about Paul, Titus, and the Corinthians, we find that it tends toward abstraction: a "prolonged absence," makes Paul "upset," worried about his "instructions." Eliminate the abstractions, add some vivid verbs, and the passage begins to take on some life:

> *Corinth soured his stomach. Paul had put his most recent letter in the hand of Titus and bustled him off. Days ticked off the calendar, and no Titus. Paul wondered how his words had gone over. But now he rejoiced in the coming of Titus.*

Again, note that the sentence structure changes and takes on even more variety. Paul's "upset" becomes localized in his belly. The "prolonged absence" is pictured as days on a calendar. "Instructions" is simplified. The verbs "soured" and "bustled" add action and color.

Finding ways to change abstract language into concrete can be great fun for the preacher, but this language also has an important homiletical function: listening to concrete language provides appropriate work for the listener. Concrete language, particularly the use of metaphor, gives the listener an enjoyable gap to fill. How much better to enliven the sermon with words that float before our eyes and make us smile. This is often the difference between the typical and the exceptional sermon. The preacher may routinely say, "The uncertainly of modern life is not always apparent," but it would be much more effective to say, "You may think that you've got it made — a paycheck, a pension, retirement in ten years. Then you get to the office and find the doors chained shut; the sign says, 'Out of Business.' " Few will relate to the first sentence, and many will brush it off as a typical pulpit bromide. The second sentence evokes thoughts, images, and emotions.

Contrast the two paragraphs below. The first is true, Christian, but abstractly dull. The second says much the same thing as the first but uses concrete, vivid language and also allows the listener more time to grasp the message:

> *As Christians, we need no longer be subject to sin which enslaves us. We can appropriate the new life of grace.*
>
> *We're free from sin. We don't have to live in chains. We can move out of the slave quarters and into the big house. We're free. The house is renovated, the carpet laid, the walls painted, the closets empty. The new life. All we have to do is move in.*

Which sermon would you rather listen to?

This last example also shows how point of view can be an effective tool in the sermon. In the first paragraph, Christians are spoken of remotely, as the kind of people who "appropriate" things. The second paragraph is more vivid in part because the perspective has changed; the preacher now speaks of Christians with a great deal of immediacy — "we" have lost our chains and moved into the big, renovated house. In the first paragraph, we stand at a distance looking far away, but in the second paragraph we are right in the middle of the action.

Point of view can sometimes be varied to produce interesting results. To make one last revision to the hypothetical sermon on 2

Corinthians, a slight change of perspective will bring the listeners much closer to the story:

> *Corinth soured his stomach. Paul had put his most recent letter in the hand of Titus and bustled him off. Days ticked off the calendar. Where was Titus? Did the church at Corinth show him the door? Did they stand up and cheer? But now — look, rejoice! Here comes Titus up the walk.*

The previous revision remains untouched until the fourth sentence, where the sermon changes from speaking about Paul to speaking in Paul's voice. The listener moves ever so slightly to identify with Paul. This revision has the advantage that it creates several new visual images, not only of a ponderous Paul anxiously awaiting his friend, but of two possible scenes in Corinth and a final image of Titus strolling up to the house. The hearers will easily jump the gap between the outside perspective and the inside one and will probably enjoy it. I must caution, however, that this device must be used sparingly, lest the hearers be overwhelmed; the preacher had probably best not jump into Titus' shoes when he gives his report to Paul.

Leading With The Heart, Leading With The Head: Story In The Sermon

No discussion of the language of a sermon would be complete without mentioning the preacher's most powerful tool, the story. In recent years the dominant vogue in homiletics has been to produce sermons that abound in bright, vivid stories, often of a personal nature, usually highly metaphorical; sometimes such sermons will be merely a string of such stories, and other times a single story will serve as the sermon. The "story sermon," or what some call "narrative preaching" (though this term is used in several other ways), often seeks to break the stronghold of rationalism on the theology and proclamation of the church. The experience of God, the argument goes, cannot be reduced to theological propositions. God must be experienced, and the stories in and of the sermon help the hearers experience God at work in the world. Stories approach the hearer indirectly, inviting the listeners into the story before striking the message home, and so overcome the resistance to the gospel inherent in our secular culture.

I do not particularly object to any of this reasoning, and I certainly enjoy a story sermon that makes effective use of narrative's power. I have been struck, however, by the number of preaching students I have had over the years who, far from finding their resistance overcome and their eyes opened, find these story sermons absolutely incomprehensible. One student persistently analyzed and reanalyzed a story sermon that used the colors red and gold to symbolize death and resurrection; the student could in fact tell me what the symbolism meant, but when I said, "That's right," he still replied, "I don't get it." This was not an isolated incident; I had many students who, curiously enough, had often been in engineering or other technical professions before their seminary careers, who were genuinely baffled by highly metaphorical sermons that seemed quite obvious to me.

I have concluded that the reason some people become engineers or sit at desks with columns of figures, while others go into sales or other people-oriented professions, is that some people lead with the heart while others lead with the head. Those who are extroverts or who respond first and foremost to people may well find the dynamic, personal imagery of the story sermon truly a liberation from dry, lifeless dogma. For others, perhaps introverts, certainly more stimulated by ideas, dry dogma may be the spice of life. Some who grow up on arid doctrinal sermons find the story sermon a wonderful breath of fresh air; others consider it simply an oddity.

Stories do not necessarily in and of themselves provide guidance for their own interpretation. True, sometimes the story preacher wants the story to stand on its own, and sometimes one can do nothing else. Certainly a good story needs no ham-handed explanation appended to it; if it worked, it worked, but if not, get on with the rest of the sermon. Still, stories must be framed, and they must be told a certain way. Sometimes they call out for a summary. Interpretation may be built into how and when a story is told. Interpretive clues can be scattered in among the stories. Sometimes the story can be buttressed with a plain statement of purpose without violating the grandeur of the form. If the stories are to convey the gospel, they must be given a place within the gospel. Over several months or years, a series of entirely uninterpreted stories becomes as arid as the heaviest dogmatic tome, because the people have gained no context for interpretation. The stories stand simply as nice stories, not heralds to the gospel. The listeners, if they are to see the gospel in the stories, need clues only the preacher can give. In essence, a string of story sermons may in the long run prove too great a gap for a congregation to span.

Preachers should be aware of their preferences and the preferences of their congregations: do we lead with the heart or the head? Those who lead with the head may want to experiment with storytelling, though if my former engineers are any indication, metaphor may prove beyond the reach of some. Pure storytellers should realize that while a congregation can adjust to this style over a period of time, they will need help in understanding this new style. Sometimes this preacher may find occasion to use another style of preaching. As always, the unremitting repetition of one form can make even the most imaginative preacher seem to be saying the same thing over and over again.

While both hearers and preachers will have preferences in the use of stories, images, and explanation, I believe that on some level we need both. The pictures invoked by stories help create a world, something explanation cannot do on its own; however, explanation provides rationale and gives guidance for interpreting the stories. For instance, in one of the examples I used above, both explanation and a story-like metaphor stand side by side:

> *We're free from sin. We don't have to live in chains. We can move out of the slave quarters and into the big house. We're free. The house is renovated, the carpet laid, the walls painted, the closets empty. The new life. All we have to do is move in.*

The main part of the section uses a metaphor to describe the Christian life. But the section begins with a simple statement: "We're free from sin." This statement gives guidance for the hearers, who now know how to fill in the metaphoric gap.

Not every story is a good story for the sermon. We have all been subjected to the trivial pulpit jokes that embarrass the hearers and trivialize the gospel. The preacher should exercise discernment in telling a story, humorous or otherwise. Stories must always support the purpose of the sermon without strain. The popularity of story sermons has perhaps created the impression that every sermon must have a story, in the mistaken belief that dull abstraction and arid argument are the only alternatives. The sermon that uses oral language well may never need a story, its bright verbs and tangible nouns working better than the story that must be stretched to fit.

Another questionable trend is the prevalence of personal stories in story sermons. Personal stories come in two varieties, those in which the narrator is the focus of the story, and those in which the focus is elsewhere. I have little objection to the latter, but the inevitable narcissicistic overtones of the first type may well disqualify it from use in the pulpit. This kind of first-person narrative may also be inherently manipulative. It calls for a response, and that response is to a large degree a response to a person, not a sermon. I recall a classroom sermon in which a student told of a deeply personal problem that was obviously a matter for counseling but not an appropriate topic for the pulpit. Yet the other students reacted with overwhelming enthusiasm — how could they not? To reject the sermon would have been to reject their friend and colleague, and they were already too well trained as pastors to ignore a soul in need. A positive response was the only possible response without incurring personal animosity. It is hard to see how a story which makes the preacher the focus can avoid either asking for the congregation's admiration or the congregation's care. Either the preacher stands as a hero or pleads for understanding in the midst of failure. In either case, it is hard to turn the focus from the messenger back to the message.

Some preachers will object that their personal stories have produced overwhelming congregational response — my point, exactly. Our job is not to evoke an emotional response but to preach the gospel. The cost of the personal story may be too high. Even if the focus is not precisely on the preacher's success or failure, there is a risk in talking about oneself, because the personal spotlight may obscure the gospel. Any time the preacher tells a personal story, the preacher must weigh that story in light of the risk: what does the story reveal about me, and will that distract from my message? Sometimes the risk is worth it, and other times it is not. Sometimes the story must be told and can be told no other way. Fortunately, most stories from personal experience can be couched in the third person with little or nothing lost, and if the congregation nudges the preacher afterward with a knowing smile and says, "We knew all along that it was you!" the preacher has not invited inappropriate response; they have filled that gap for themselves.[11]

These cautions aside, the language of stories is oral language, congenial to the sermon, precisely because it is vivid and concrete. Stories are about people who do things, who go places, who have interesting adventures. Stories work well in sermons because they draw pictures in the minds of the hearers. When carefully crafted to be well-focused and concise, they are powerful purveyors of the gospel.

On Metaphor

Metaphor, like its close cousin, simile, is an important adjunct to storytelling. Metaphor takes advantage of an important feature of storytelling that is also the essence of oral communication: the concrete noun. Nouns like "Father," "Mother," "bread," "wine," "boat," "wind," and "sea" assist the preacher not just in their ease of use and simplicity of acceptance but also in the chameleonic ability to say more than they say. They not only draw pictures in the mind but can also easily come to symbolize something important about our life. The concrete noun can take on great conceptual power without tossing aside the virtues of its specificity. Our language about God is inherently metaphoric; we cannot look on the true face of the Lord and live, and so we can describe the divine only in terms of earthly shadows. So it is not surprising that metaphor lends itself so well to our preaching. Metaphor aids the preacher in establishing both meaning and interest, giving the listener an important gap to fill.

This is not to say that all metaphor is good metaphor in the sermon. One unfortunate result of the emphasis on narrative imagery is the overelaboration of metaphor. Traditional homiletics, of course, was far from immune from this fault; someone once (as a joke) sent me a tape of a sermon on Philippians 3:2, "Beware of the dogs," which listed thirteen different kinds of dogs one should beware of, from the hound dog who pokes his nose into your business to the poodle who puts herself on display. The danger becomes more acute the more the sermon depends on metaphor. In the example above about the slave quarters, the preacher probably is safe, but if he strays from the big house and starts wandering the grounds of the plantation, no telling what may happen. Metaphor soon becomes allegory, which usually leaves everyone confused. The overelaborated metaphor runs the danger of saying too much and thus losing whatever meaning it began with. Also, the more a metaphor is elaborated, the more likely it is to acquire unwanted associations or even to become a mixed metaphor, which can have disastrous (though sometimes hilarious) unintentional results. If I leave the big house to join Scarlet and Prissy in Atlanta, I trivialize the gospel and invite jokes about Clark Gable as the Messiah.

Many metaphors are best left alone to do their work and not elaborated. For example, I once used these lines in a sermon about self-righteousness:

> *Be careful where you point your finger, especially when you stand on the edge of the garbage can and lean over to point down, because that edge is razor-sharp, and it's awful hard to keep your balance. Awful hard.*

The razor-sharp garbage can did its work well, and I can attest that it stayed with many of the hearers for a long time. It worked because of its brevity and its shock value. To elaborate further would have ruined it; garbage cans are not razor-sharp, and no one would really try to stand on one.

The preacher who makes use of metaphor must also be willing to give up the illusion of control. This is actually an illusion all preachers had best forgo; there is really no way to prevent misinterpretation. The preacher may try hard to clarify and reiterate, but ultimately nothing can prevent hearers' minds wandering and their ears skipping a beat, or ensure that each person knows and understands the precise definition and connotation of each word. One man was surprised to hear himself congratulated on a political race he did not win; the headline read, "Jones not elected for council," but not everyone saw the "not." When I left parish life for graduate school, my boss announced that "Bill Shepherd is leaving," and then went on to say many kind things about "Bill." The problem was that there was another staff member of that church named "Bill," a rather bookish fellow himself, and half the congregation, hearing only the first name, thought of him rather than me. Every preacher knows that occasionally someone will say, "What you said meant so much to me," and then wipe the smile off your face when the admirer rattles off something with only the vaguest connection to that sermon you worked so hard on. Misinterpretation is a fact of communication and in and of itself precludes the notion of control in the pulpit.

This is especially the case with metaphor, which by its very nature opens itself up to multiple interpretations. With metaphor, one cannot really even speak of misinterpretation, precisely because many interpretations are possible. For example, I have often quoted to friends this line: "Marriage is a little boat made of a twig, a leaf, and a wadded-up piece of gum."[12] One friend responded, "Yes, it is fragile, isn't it." Another friend replied that after ten years, his marriage was at least a rowboat with a servicable motor. The variations have not only to do with the hearers' verbal ability, but also with their perception of marriage; one recently divorced will hear the line differently from one never married, or one married fifty years. The preacher who uses metaphor must let the metaphor do its work; to control it is hopeless. As the Russian proverb says, "Once a word is spoken, it flies, you can't catch it." At least one of the meanings of this metaphorical gem is that the one who utters a word cannot control the hearers' interpretation of that word.

Still, metaphor and simile are important and useful tools for the preacher. Carefully, skillfully chosen metaphors will add a good deal of life to the pulpit; the preacher in search of good models can look to the best fiction for guidance. Metaphors in sermons, like stories, are best governed by taste and discernment.

The Bible And Oral Language

As with formal structures, the Bible itself is a good source of vivid oral language. Jesus regularly spoke of concrete, everyday items such as bread, coins, and lamps. His stories were populated with real men and women, not abstract "humankind." Paul too is a master of oral style, having learned to read and write in the rhetorical styles of his day. Of course, not all biblical language avoids abstraction, and there are some terms and concepts that are quite alien to the modern mind. The preacher must sometimes engage in a balancing act, bringing instruction without obfuscation. However, as I have already argued, the purpose of the sermon is to transform the modern world in light of the biblical one. Where we can take our words directly from the biblical text, we will be most effective at enticing our hearers into the biblical tradition, so that the tradition soaks into modern reality.

The Bible is also a primary source of stories. While some may lament the biblical illiteracy of the masses, others will take the challenge to tell and retell the biblical stories. No, we cannot expect everyone to remember the story of Gideon or Job, assuming they have heard these stories; recall is too short a memory phenomenon, and there is already too much to remember in this age of information. Rather than beat people over the head with their memory lapses, why not refresh their memories? A biblical story told carefully and vividly will leave them on the edge of their seats, and as the details accumulate they may well recognize it as a story they have heard before. Bible stories need not be couched in somber King James diction. They are about real human beings who, for all their cultural distinction, think, love, hate, and act much like their descendants through the ages. If the story needs updating, then update it; the congregation will be amused to find Martha at the microwave and Mary taking notes on her notebook computer. If the energy spent on the average story sermon were applied to revitalizing the old, old stories, there would be little to complain of in terms of biblical illiteracy. The same goes for the classical tales of Shakespeare or other authors; we need not limit our stories to modern personal anecdotes. The classic stories are classics because of their enduring value, and their enduring value lies in their ability to pinpoint the essence of humanity.

Retelling the old, old story is an activity that lies close to the heart of my argument. Christians need the Bible if they are going to live in a new reality. The biblical stories and images are sharp and powerful, able to enter the modern world and transform it in their own image. Together with the more discursive biblical forms such as Paul's letters or the wisdom literature, and the more poetic forms from Psalms or Revelation, biblical stories form the foundation of our faith. The Bible does speak to the heart as well as the head. Christians who hear the Bible regularly will gradually find that their world is a different, more biblical world. This is the task of the sermon. Biblical storytelling is one of its most powerful tools.

Conclusion

The sermon as an oral text uses form and language to create gaps appropriate to its nature. The listeners, as "readers" of this text, work with the text to fill in these gaps and create meaning. For the preacher, the goal of this oral presentation is ultimately to create a new world infused with the power of the gospel.

Why does a preacher make creative use of form and language, forsaking the abstractions of theological truth to speak of a world that can be seen, touched, and smelled? Not just to be interesting or amusing, but because worlds are concrete things. A "world" is a way of looking at and putting together the things we can see, touch, and smell. We live in concrete reality, not among abstractions. The Bible itself contains stories and images as well as arguments, and we need all of these if our world is to be transformed by them. A sermon that lives without tangible items may suggest an interesting idea, but it will never by itself give birth to a new world. The world of the sermon is as real as you and me.

1. Craddock, *Preaching,* pp. 84-85.

2. My first choice among textbooks is Craddock's *Preaching*. A good alternative or supplement is Thomas Long's *The Witness of Preaching* (Louisville: Westminster/John Knox Press, 1989). Advanced students can learn much from Buttrick's *Homiletic*.

3. It is beyond the scope of this study to consider the manifold nonverbal communication that takes place in the sermon, involving the preacher's stance and position, clothing, gesturing, facial movements and eye contact, and so on. Suffice it to say that nonverbal communication is a servant of the verbal text and must be congruent with the form and content of the sermon's words. One does not muse while staring people in the eye, nor proclaim a decree while standing in the aisle and reading notes scribbled on tattered yellow legal paper.

4. One written convention that is often carried over into sermons is numbering. I am generally skeptical about numbering in sermons, since numbers do not in and of themselves bear meaning apart from being visually connected to words on a page. Numbers also tend to work against the unity of the sermon, the numbered points being fragmented as separate entities rather than integrated into an ongoing movement. If care is given to arrange the sermon so that one point flows into another, the preacher can dispense with numbers in favor of words and increase clarity all around.

5. Buttrick, *Homiletic,* pp. 38-39.

6. See Craddock, *Preaching,* pp. 214-216, and Long, *Witness of Preaching,* pp. 181-188.

7. See Craddock, *Preaching,* pp. 176-189, and Long, *Witness of Preaching,* pp. 92-132.

8. Craddock, *Preaching,* pp. 165-168.

9. See Walter J. Ong, *Orality and Literacy: The Technologizing of the Word,* New Accents (New York: Methuen, 1982); Werner H. Kelber, *The Oral and Written Gospel: The Hermeneutics of Speaking and Writing in the Synoptic Tradition, Mark, Paul, and Q* (Philadelphia: Fortress Press, 1983); Stephen D. Moore, *Literary Criticism and the Gospels: The Theoretical Challenge* (New Haven: Yale University Press, 1989), pp. 84-88.

10. Craddock, *Preaching,* pp. 177-180. See also Thomas G. Long, *Preaching and the Literary Forms of the Bible* (Philadelphia: Fortress Press, 1989).

11. I might add here that the overwhelming opinion of my students who had grown up as preacher's kids was that they did not appreciate having their lives used as sermon illustrations. The one exception was an inveterate extrovert who noted that his father had always asked permission before telling stories about the family.

    While families may or may not release their stories, the confidences of counseling and confession are inviolate to the Nth generation. No church will trust a pastor who blabs about the people who come for care, even if that care was offered long ago in another church.

12. The line comes from a novel by Amy Herrick, *At the Sign of the Naked Waiter* (New York: HarperCollins, 1992).

Chapter 5

Reading The Sermon

My old Methodist preacher friend likes to tell this story. A young aspirant to the pulpit came to see the wise old pastor. "I've studied theology," said the youngster. "I've worked at biblical studies, ethics, church history, and pastoral theology. All this study, and I don't know what to say in my first sermon. What shall I preach about?" The wise old pastor thought for a while, and then said, "You shall preach about God, and you shall preach about twenty minutes."

Over the years I have come to think that there is a great deal of wisdom in what is, even my friend admits, a pretty bad joke. I do not refer to the time limit, but to the subject matter: the sermon is about God. This may seem an elemental statement, but sometimes the obvious is the least apparent truth. The young preacher in the joke was so overwhelmed by the theological curriculum that this most basic truth had been covered up. Add to this the homiletic prescription that the preacher not rehearse the seminary curriculum in the pulpit, but talk about the everyday lives of real people, and the sermon quickly becomes a busy place. The huge cast of characters, the profound rush of ideas, and the press of urgent need may sometimes crowd out the star. Many preachers, young and old, scramble to integrate their studies into a message that is new and interesting but not necessarily about God. Others work so hard to be "relevant" that the primary subject of the sermon gets lost in a maze of stories, quotes, and wit. The net result is a sermon that perhaps speaks delightfully about the life and times of the preacher's Uncle Al, or perhaps speaks profoundly about the present state of social or political affairs, but speaks only dimly and in parables about our ultimate concern. To judge from the many sermons I have heard over the years, the Sunday sermon often proves to be more about us than God.

I have titled this final chapter "Reading the Sermon" as a way of extending the argument I have been making throughout this book: there are many different kinds of texts and many different kinds of reading. We have talked about what it means to be readers of biblical texts and how readers themselves are (in a sense) texts that need understanding. We have seen how the sermon itself is a powerful text, a word that is also a deed. We now will "read" the sermon, that is, step back and interpret preaching itself — why we do what we do. This has been a book about rethinking the sermon, and in this final chapter I would like to think twice about the preacher's ultimate goal. As a way of getting at the subject, I will deal at length in this chapter with one critic of present-day preaching, Edward Farley, and indicate the degree to which my ideas overlap his, and the places where he and I differ. Farley's critique of what he calls the "bridge paradigm" of preaching is instructive for all who would find a new way for the sermon.

A reading of the sermon will remind us of the goal of all our work. We do not study congregations, biblical texts, and their interaction merely to earn our paychecks or to further institutional goals. Stories, images, and arguments do not exist solely for themselves, nor for our audiences. We are not, despite many claims to the contrary, in the entertainment business. We serve not ourselves, nor our congregations, but a higher power. A reading of the sermon will show that the point is simply to talk about God.

Preaching Bible vs. Preaching Gospel

Note that I did not say, "the point of it all is to talk about the Bible." The sermon is not, ultimately, about the Bible. This may seem like a strange assertion in a book about biblical preaching, but in making this statement I do not revoke anything I have said up to this point. Nor am I repeating what I have said earlier about the pulpit being no place for the technical language of biblical studies. My point here is that we do not preach the Bible *per se*. The Bible is a means to an end, not the goal itself. The sermon is about the God the Bible portrays.

A Critique Of Biblical Preaching: Edward Farley

Preaching manuals have sometimes missed this point: the sermon first and foremost is about God, not about the Bible. One recent critic, Edward Farley, has gone so far as to say that the homiletic obsession with the Bible has obscured the sermon's focus and given the preacher an impossible task.[1] Farley has correctly noted that, as usually taught in the seminaries, what is preached is the Bible or the biblical message. More than that, since the Bible is divided into small units for liturgical use, what is preached is a specific passage that is to be worked over in great depth by the preacher. Something in this passage must prove preachable — somehow the lection must become fertile ground for a message of consolation, hope, transformation, or prophetic provocation. As Farley points out, homileticians and preachers outside evangelical and fundamentalist churches foreswear "proof-texting," so the biblical material likely to be present in or contribute to the sermon is limited to the passages prescribed by the liturgy. The preacher who works this way, and Farley suggests that it has been the dominant homiletical model for some time, deals for the most part with the Bible as it is divided into lections. This way of working encourages a particular view of biblical authority. Since the Bible is present to preaching only in these shorter passages, the preacher must assume that each passage contains a Word from God. Despite the disdain for proof-texting, small biblical units taken out of historical and literary context take on great authority.

Further, according to Farley, this dominant model of preaching demands that the preacher discover a certain kind of link between the Word of God gleaned from the passage of the day and the situation of the congregation. Since the sermon is delivered in a liturgical setting to a particular congregation, the sermon must take into account the historical, social, political, economic, and pastoral situation of that gathered audience. This means that each sermon must link the complexities of a particular brief biblical passage to the complexities of the life of a particular congregation. The dominant homiletic model, says Farley, relies heavily on analogy to provide that link. Not only must there be something preachable in each lection, but there must be a legitimate analogy between whatever is preachable there and the situation of the congregation, and the preacher must discover and exploit this analogy.

Thus Farley speaks of this view of preaching, which he sees as deeply rooted in Protestant consciousness, as "the bridge paradigm":

> *The paradigm here can be expressed in the form of a metaphor of building a bridge. The preacher's task is to build a bridge from that which is preached (the truth of the specific passage) to the situation of the congregation. The construction of the crafted written sermon sets the problem of traversing the bridge.*[2]

The result of all this work is usually a written manuscript, to be presented orally, that uses argument, metaphor, and narrative to bring together the concerns of the biblical lection and the congregation.

But, according to Farley, there are some fatal flaws in the bridge paradigm. First, it is a departure from the primitive preaching portrayed in the New Testament. There, says Farley, drawing mainly on Paul, what is preached is not the content of scripture passages, but the message of Christ crucified. Second, dealing with the Bible only as lectionary units results in an atomizing of scriptural books that in Farley's view actually casts a shroud over the scriptures, as the search for small nuggets of life's lessons week after week becomes oblivious to the grand beauty of the biblical books when seen as a whole. Third, as we have already seen, sometimes specific biblical texts contain abhorrent ideas or images and so are not read in church; that these passages can be omitted by lectionaries merely proves the weakness of the procedure — picking a brief passage for preaching does not and cannot work across the board.

Most importantly, according to Farley, the preacher working under the bridge paradigm faces an impossible task. The quest for a preachable something that has an analogy in the life of the congregation is doomed from the beginning. By and large the biblical texts were not designed for such use. Any biblical passage short enough to be read in church is part of a larger whole. There is no guarantee that any particular passage will contain a preachable truth, and even if it does it is part of a whole not readily accessible to the hearers. "There is nothing about arbitrarily selected passages of the Bible that in some necessary or *a priori* way contains that-which-is-proclaimed," says Farley.[3] The vast diversity of biblical passages makes it unlikely that each will provide that preachable something; it is a dubious proposition that every passage will contain, in and of itself, good tidings. Preachers usually find themselves unable to wring the preachable out of the passage by the rules of scholarly exegesis, so the passage becomes merely a jumping-off place for the sermon: "The preacher must kill the passage in order to preach on it."[4] The church has moved from preaching the gospel to preaching biblical passages, and the result is utter confusion and frustration.

Farley notes various attempts at correction — some homileticians urge preachers to do more rigorous exegesis, or to make use of rhetorical and literary studies of the Bible, or to take into account recent trends in interpretive theory that belie a simple approach to either scripture or congregation. However, Farley sees these as mere bandaids that cannot heal a severely wounded way of thinking. It is the bridge paradigm itself which is the problem. Farley holds that the preacher is summoned to preach the gospel, not biblical passages. To do so, homiletics must begin to practice "preaching minus the bridge paradigm."[5]

Beyond The Bridge Paradigm: A Response To Farley

It may seem at first glance that Farley has mounted an assault on the kind of preaching I have promoted in this book. I have suggested that biblical lections and congregations be read in equal depth, and that both be taken into account in preparing the sermon. I have argued that thorough critical study of a biblical passage will result in something "preachable" because it inevitably culminates in an encounter with otherness. I have insisted that the sermon not only speak the language of the congregation, but identify with their concerns.

Yet I find myself agreeing in many ways with Farley's argument, particularly his critique of mainstream homiletical theory. There is something rotten in the pulpit, and the fault is not merely that of a few unskilled practitioners. Take the following example: the text is Luke 13:34, "Jerusalem, Jerusalem, the city that kills the prophets and stones those who are sent to it! How often have I desired to gather your children together as a hen gathers her brood under her wings, and you were not willing!" The preacher has been taught to look for an analogy between the text and modern life. Sit back, relax, and let the images come: birds, feathery creatures — I've got it! The preacher begins to scribble. Sunday morning, he has to admit from the pulpit that he knows very little about hens (except perhaps at the end of a knife and fork). He does, however, know something about pheasant, which look a lot like hens. There follows a story about a childhood home and the woods out back, where Mama Pheasant and Babies Pheasant can be seen marching in single file. You see, says the preacher, Mama Pheasant can say two things to her brood: "Come," and "Follow me." Which, it turns out, is exactly what Jesus has to say to us today — and so on.

What is wrong here? The preacher has followed the prescribed homiletical method with care: he has sought and exploited an analogy. But were we to use the metaphor of the "bridge" to describe the transition from text to sermon, we would look back from the far shore of the sermon to see a strange sight. The bridge we have just crossed is a roller coaster, full of twists, loop-the-loops, and curlicues between here and there. On the other side, we see the scribes and the Pharisees, Herod and Jerusalem, Luke and the people of God. In between them and us, we have with us a flock of birds who talk like Jesus. Somewhere the riches of the Lukan text — which include the Lukan theme of the prophet's fated journey to Jerusalem and the resistence of the people to God's visitation — not to mention the hot theological issues that might be evoked by that text — of possible anti-Semitism in the New Testament, for example, or biblical images of a divine female — have been lost. We even lost the chicken. The bridge veered early and sharply, swiftly skirting the outspread wings of mother hen to meet pheasant from the woods, and from there to Jesus. Our heads spinning, we get off the roller coaster, not sure how we got from there to here. Come back next week; there will be another ride.

What we have here is less a demonstration of one preacher's shortcomings than a cry for help. It is symptomatic of a failed paradigm. Similarly, sermons on the "Windows of Motherhood" or the feeding of the five thousand as the miracle of sharing are not so much aberrations as unintentional parodies; such sermons take normal homiletical procedure and puff it up to elephantine proportions. The truth is that preachers quite often find themselves groping futilely for an acceptable bridge from lection to congregation, and sometimes the thinnest pretext is the only thing that will preach. One learns from long hard experience that intense, laborious exegesis will rarely yield an acceptable analogy. Better to meditate on a single surface image and follow the imaginative paths to which it leads. If those paths lead away from the biblical text, so be it. We already know that heading back towards the text will result only in frustration.

In short, preachers have been working an unworkable scheme. They have tried to exegete a useful analogy from the historical depths of the text and too often failed. More often, success can be had on the surface. The biblical text becomes a pretext, a jumping-off point. Farley's critique of the "bridge paradigm" is to this extent devastatingly accurate.

Where I find myself primarily disagreeing with Farley is in his proposed solution. Farley suggests that we preach the gospel rather than the Bible, and that is all well and true. But what, specifically, are preachers to do with the Bible once they have given up preaching on it? Farley's critique of the way we use the Bible in the pulpit doesn't get at the heart of the problem, nor suggest more appropriate ways to make use of biblical texts. In the end I believe that Farley throws the baby out with the bath.

Besides, I see what Farley calls "bridge paradigm" in a quite different perspective. Yes, it is the dominant homiletic model, and yes, it is a problem. I believe, however, that we will better understand its shortcomings once we look at the roots of its dominance. The bridge paradigm is in fact the dominant homiletical model because it springs from a dominant theological model. This kind of preaching is deeply rooted in the theological presuppositions of experiential-expressivism, what I have called "Religion Feels." You will recall that under this view of religion the essence of the human encounter with the divine is experiential. One has certain religious feelings or impulses, and it is from these feelings that religious ritual and theological language spring. Religious experience on this view is a constant across time and culture; the types of religious experience available to us today are pretty much the same as that at hand for Buddha or the Apostle Paul.

The essence of the "bridge paradigm" of preaching is in fact the essence of "Religion Feels." The preacher is looking in both biblical text and in congregational experience for the same thing: some sort of religiousness. Such religiousness is found in experience, in the feeling that the divine is present. Since this feeling is constant across the ages, it should be no problem to find the religious experience underlying the biblical text and translate it into modern terms. Preaching becomes no more than what Harry Emerson Fosdick called a simple "engineering operation," where the riches of biblical experience are transferred across time and culture to modern people.[6] The experiential-expressivist, "Religion Feels" approach, in keeping with a tendency to see all biblical texts as allegories about their authors, allows only for analogy as a way of spanning the gap between then and now. If one can find an exact analogy to the original historical situation, one can preach the text properly; Paul's battle with gnostics becomes our battle with the New Age, while Matthew's persecuted church becomes a model for our dwindling, beleaguered congregation.

Since religious experience is on this view basically the same for everyone, this view of preaching poses no theoretical problems. However, as Farley points out, the resulting sermons have produced few satisfied customers. I belive that the failure of this homiletical model can be traced back to its theological roots. I have already shown in Chapter Three the problem that lies in the presuppositions of experiential-expressivism: one simply cannot assume that all religious experience is the same. That preaching on the "bridge paradigm" has proved to be frustrating for the preacher and infertile ground for the listener is testimony to the failure of "Religion Feels."

The search for analogy on the "Religion Feels" model dictates the work that goes on in the preacher's study. Farley correctly sees the impossibility of the task. To wring a preachable moral for the day out of every biblical lection is difficult, even more so if analogy is the sole thing preachable. The need to discover a spot to build the bridge becomes the focus of the preacher's preparation; it determines how the biblical passage is studied. The search for that preachable something dictates the terms of the search itself; nonsensical goals lead to nonsensical practice. If one is looking for an analogy between the text and the congregation as a place for bridge-building, one will find such an analogy, and probably no more. If one can look only for analogy, analogy is what one will find, however tenuous it may be. Such study, being reduced to one rather limited object, is indeed an impoverishment.

The need for a bridge is unique to the "Religion Feels" approach. Propositionalism, or "Religion Thinks," allows for no gap between text and reader; the propositionalist preacher moves straight across an eternal verity. The cultural-linguistic, or "Religion Does," approach, which I have been advocating, allows for greater freedom and a looser approach to biblical studies. One need not search for eternal verities nor historical analogies, but is free to explore all aspects of the text. The preacher who studies the text critically in search not of analogy but, as I have suggested, in search of otherness is in a different place entirely. Abandon the search for analogy and the terms of weekly biblical study change dramatically. Thus Farley is wrong to see recent trends in contemporary homiletics, which point towards new views of how we interpret texts, as merely a fix of the failed bridge paradigm. He fails to see that the presuppositions of recent literary, rhetorical, and hermeneutical theories are incompatible with the old way of looking at preaching; to follow them is to abandon "Religion Feels" and the "bridge paradigm" in favor of a "Religion Does" position.

Attention to the complex interactions between texts and readers changes the way we think about the sermon. One cannot continue to see reading and preaching in simplistic terms. Many interpretive moves are possible, not just the "bridge." Given a gulf to span, one may find in the passage not a bridge but a dam, a levee, a ferry, an ocean liner, a helicopter, or even a leisurely swim — that is to say, simple analogy is not the only link between an ancient text and modern life. The possible analogy between ourselves and the original historical situation is only one aspect of the text. The Bible contains stories, poetry, proverbs, images, and arguments.

The form and content itself is meaningful, not just our appropriation of the text or our search for common ground. As we read and relate to the stories, arguments, and images of biblical people, those people and their lives become a part of our lives. As symbols they come in and do their work on us and give the Bible a transforming power. Biblical texts become a part of the way we think about life, not distant analogies that have to be transported, however awkwardly. Reading and interpreting biblical texts in this light proves to be a more complicated task than "building a bridge." The biblical texts themselves begin to resist simplistic "translations" into modern life, tending instead to take over and transform that life. Reading the Bible, both in and of itself and as part of the sermon, creates a new world, not merely a bridge between two existing entities. While there are no doubt gaps between ancient texts and modern churches, the gaps are such that metaphors such as the "bridge" or "translation" prove inadequate analogies. I do not suggest that we put a bandaid on the bridge; I suggest we look for other metaphors.

Preachers will thrive on regular critical study of biblical texts when conceived in this broader dimension, but such breadth cannot be achieved without work, and it cannot be done in the abstract. Thus the preacher must study individual passages of the Bible. Here is my main disagreement with Farley: the preacher cannot abandon the study of specific biblical texts. Farley wishes the Bible to be present in the sermon in its "many and rich dimensions":

> *The preacher can draw from the world of Bible stories (Nathan's rebuke of David), symbols (covenant, kingdom, messiah), metaphors (shepherding, light, the law court), social realities (ecclesia), comparisons (faith as it is expressed in Jesus' teaching and in Romans), moral insight (Paul on idolatry), and editorial slants (Luke on the poor).*[7]

It is hard to see, however, how the busy pastor will be led into these larger themes apart from a regular and disciplined encounter with specific biblical texts. Sermon preparation provides not only a built-in weekly deadline for the procrastinator, but also numerous points at which to enter the wider world of scripture. The preacher once freed of the desperate search for analogy can pursue the thread found lying loose in one passage as far as it will go. Studying specific lections is a way of getting at the broader dimensions of the Bible that can be uncovered only with persistent and careful reading. To encourage preachers not to deal with specific passages is to set them loose without the grip on reality that particularity offers. One may soon find that the Bible is taken even less seriously than before: vague abstractions and watered-down remembrances of seminary lectures replace the vivid encounter with something recently learned. Only regular, serious, specific biblical study gives preachers the resources the sermon calls for. We preachers need concrete encounter with otherness if we are going to give our congregations the same.

Grace And The Interpretive Community

Farley, in suggesting that critical theories of reading are mere bandaids to a failed method, fails himself to take into account the wider reading process: we read in light of the whole. If reading is truly a function of interpretive communities, then the broader context in which a community lives comes into play in any reading, no matter how small we slice scripture. This is why preachers have persisted in preaching the gospel, and even preaching well, using flawed models. Instinctively, the reader corrects for the inadequacy of theory. The gut feeling of many preachers and congregations is that any particular biblical lection must be understood in light of the whole counsel of God. Farley is wrong precisely where he is right: we read the Bible in light of the gospel, and we need the Bible as the concrete expression of that gospel. It goes to the essence of who we — both preachers and congregation — are as readers.

When concern for the reading process is seen as a new fitting — rather than a cheap fix, duct tape on old pipes — we can begin to see the ways the interpretive community specifies that texts be read and how this reading relates to preaching. As has long been noted, there is no interpretation without presuppositions. All texts contain gaps, and all interpretive communities promote certain ways of filling those gaps. Perhaps the most important gaps involve the broader point of view of the community: ultimately, what do we think is going on here? How is the world put together, and what is our place in it? In preaching, the church will provide these presuppositions. The church sees the world as a place drenched with God's grace, and humanity's place as those who respond one way or another to what is offered by the Other. Any reader working within this worldview will search for traces of that grace.

Between the text and the sermon is an imaginative filter of grace. The preacher reads in light of grace. Every biblical text is understood in light of the whole, and the whole tells of an Other who offers otherness as a gift. The primary gap encountered throughout the scriptures is the gap between our human understanding and God's love. Left to ourselves, we find what we think of as life in that which is created. Fortunately for us, we find that creation resists being mistaken for the Creator. Our fellow creatures prove to be outside our control. We are thus reminded again and again that our wishes and desires are subject to a higher power. We are constantly moving between idolatry and faith, between our tendency to put ourselves on the pedestal and God's little reminders that we are dependent. This is the overarching message of the biblical tradition, and it is the light by which any particular passage is read. As with any encounter with otherness, we must exercise discernment as we read and preach. Where we do not find grace on the surface, we must dig deeper. Grace fills the gap.

The preacher in reading biblical texts for the congregation must fill the gaps with grace if the congregation is going to be given any guidance in their own gap-filling. It is not necessarily apparent from any particular passage read on any particular day that the Bible as a whole is about God's grace. I suspect that most pewsitters, given an exposure to the Bible consisting solely of that which is read in church, would imagine just the opposite: the Bible seems to be a barrage of challenge and failure, a series of commandments given by God, a series of human failure to meet the commandments. Pewsitters are often missing the crucial piece: this human failure is symptomatic of our tendency to trust in our own ability to do what God wills, rather than put our souls in God's care. If nothing else, preaching can counter faulty impressions left by biblical texts read out of context.

For example, the beginning of Mark 7 deals with the complaint of the Pharisees that the disciples eat with unwashed hands. As it is specified in the lectionary (Proper 17, Year B), only certain verses of the passage are read (Mark 7:1-8, 14-15, 21-23), so that the congregation from the beginning receives a distorted picture: the section on the Corban offering is entirely omitted, and teaching delivered to the crowd is cast as delivered to the disciples alone. Add to this the great historical and cultural gaps between the text and modern life, gaps having to do with ritual purity and adherence to tradition, and the people end up with a very strange, resistant text. The Pharisees seem to be petty people concerned with the trivialities of the washroom; their apparent obsession with cultic purity is readily mistaken for a modern notion, based on scientific study, that one washes hands to prevent infection. Perhaps more importantly, the passage has a negative cast; it is, as read, a passage about being defiled, whether from the inside or the outside. The congregation will nod in agreement; the evils contained in the human heart, listed at length by Jesus, are indeed bad things to be avoided. They will be left with the impression, however, that there is nothing one can do about such evils, or that only bad hearts contain them, or both.

Is this passage a challenge for the preacher? Yes, and not just in terms of the cultural gap. The preacher must read it in light of the gospel, because the congregation is not likely to — the lection is simply not on the face of it amenable to interpretation as good news. Fortunately, the preacher has the advantage of deeper knowledge, due to weekly preparation. The preacher also has tools to help shape the congregation's reading of the text; in this instance, story proves a powerful gap-filling tool. Even if the Corban section is omitted by the lectionary, it still can make a fine "for instance" story in the sermon. The Pharisees, too, have a story of sorts, in their history of concern for the Law given by Moses, and their tradition of building a fence to protect that Law from violation. The preacher can fill gaps by providing the wider context and scope of the issue at hand. The issue of defiled hands opens on to the broader issue of ritual purity and from there to purity of heart. The issues in this passage are the basic issues between God and humanity: our need for a central focus (in this case symbolized by the pure heart), and our fumbling efforts to find that focus apart from God. The human failure to seek cleansing in God alone is typified in the Pharisees' attempt to build a fence around the Law; the Pharisees become people to be identified with rather than scorned. This text, despite first appearances, can indeed become a moment of grace for preacher and congregation. Its cultural strangeness and seeming resistance to positive construal are marks of its otherness. The sermon will exploit that otherness by placing the passage in its broader setting. The preacher moves the congregation from anti-bacterial scrubs through cultic purity and into a world suffused with grace.

Passages that create negative or disturbing impressions cry out for interpretation. Modern women may find themselves distressed when they are exhorted to subject themselves to males in Ephesians 5:21-33 (Proper 16, Year B). More than one preacher has seen women leave the church in a huff during the reading of this passage! The preacher who has done the homework knows that this passage is part of larger section (Ephesians 5:21—6:9). The whole passage is what biblical scholars call a "table of household duties," a common feature of Hellenistic moral philosophy. It assumes a social order quite different from the modern nuclear family; the ancient family unit was extended to include distant relatives and even slaves. This extended household functioned on a strictly patriarchal, hierarchal system of authority — orders ran from the top down. Indeed, the biblical household tables are exceptional in that they counsel Christians to operate within the system on the basis of mutuality: "Be subject to one another out of reverence for Christ" (Ephesians 5:21) stands as a heading for the whole. Seen in this cultural perspective, the household table, rather than being a support for an oppressive society, may be seen as subverting ancient and modern notions of power (and the modern idolatry of independence as well!). The preacher could go a long way toward setting this passage in context simply by extending the lectionary reading to include the entire household table, since the exhortations to husbands and wives take on a very different tone when read in light of similar stipulations between slaves and masters (Ephesians 6:5-9). A social order that commended slavery will not uncritically be taken as an infallible guide for modern gender relations.

Preaching recognizes grace as a word from outside ourselves. Yet the preacher and congregation form an interpretive community for whom grace is the essence of reading, and thus they bring grace to each passage read. It is an ironic circle of reading: we read in light of grace because we believe what we find in the Bible is grace. The irony and the circle come with membership in the interpretive community. Preaching is circular: the preacher reads a biblical text in light of and for a particular congregation, who in turn read the biblical text in light of the preacher's own reading (the sermon), and who then become the congregation for whom and in light of which the next sermon is prepared. What keeps this circle from becoming ingrown, constantly feeding on itself, is grace itself: again and again, the preacher and congregation find in their reading a message from the Other.

It is when the sermon stops living by grace that it goes astray. Here the inevitable connection between the spiritual life of the preacher and the content of the sermon becomes clear. Preachers, like everyone else, sometimes get caught in the web of idolatry; assuming that their own houses are in order, they stop living by grace and start to meddle with the spiritual lives of their congregation. Self-righteousness is the inevitable by-product of life that idolizes religion. The sermon becomes not a moment of grace but an exhortation to shape up or ship out; rather than opening the door so a crack of light can bounce into the room, the preacher berates the congregation for sitting in the dark. When the sermon takes on a tone of fussiness, when commandment and exhortation outweigh praise and wonder, when the congregation comes out of church feeling inadequate rather than blessed, then the preacher best take stock — something is out of kilter. The Spirit may be at work among the congregation, but it is hindered by resistance at the top.

Some preachers are afraid to turn the focus entirely towards God. Will we not be encouraging antinomianism, or neglecting the consequences of human failure? True, human beings do not need to be told that their actions are insignificant or to be forgiven for things they feel no guilt over. Such objections spring from a parody of life under grace and are to some extent part of the resistance to grace. If we take seriously God's role as Creator, Judge, Savior, and Redeemer, we will recognize that which we share with the Other, being created in the same image. We will not minimize the human need to be creative, nor the consequences of our actions, nor our hope that God will make things right. Human beings need to have important things to do with their lives. This does not negate grace but creates more opportunities for it; only as we confront one another with mutually-exclusive desires do we recognize our mutual dependence on God. Grace does not lessen the consequences of bad choices but helps us to learn from them and to move on in more faithful ways. To live by grace is above all to admit that we see only partially and that we have to trust God to take care of the larger picture. Meanwhile, we do act, and we act in response to the Other.[8]

Make no mistake about it, the oft-expressed fears of proclaiming "cheap grace" are overstated. Grace is never cheap, precisely because it requires that we let God work rather than doing it ourselves. Our natural human propensity is to assume that our project is God's project, that our work is God's work. Living by grace requires that we recognize the folly of such notions. To act with power and intention and yet leave control to God is truly a tightrope act. The preacher's job is to unwind strands of God's grace and spread them out for the people to see, trusting that the Spirit will take care of the messy details of opening blind eyes, deaf ears, and willful human hearts.

Conclusion: Preaching Grace

A parishioner had been sent by his company on an extended off-site job. He went unhappily but came back from the long exodus glowing. "It wasn't a job," he said, "it was a crusade." It turned out that the miserable location received only one good television signal, a 24-hour affiliate of a popular Christian broadcast network.

Provoked by the miserable working situation and coupled with an enthusiastic, "right with the Lord" roommate, this man experienced a profound spiritual transformation while watching that one television channel. Everyone in the congregation noticed that he had changed.

I was not particularly thrilled with the programming of that particular religious broadcaster, nor the fundamentalist baggage my parishioner came home with. I was and am willing, however, to forego any attempt to fix such a person, not only because it is hopeless, but because it is unnecessary. Whether the man will remain in that particular theological camp is a matter of his future growth. But more than that, I recognize that a powerful set of ideas, practices, and experiences has shaped his life. He has encountered, perhaps for the first time, a strong sense of religious love and devotion. One function of fundamentalism, as with other renewal movements, is to instill love. The man came back infected not so much with a doctrine but with the love of God.

Pastors often hear the congregation clamoring for more Bible study, only to find that when it is offered, no one shows up. This is not, as it may seem to the frustrated teacher sitting alone in the classroom, pure hypocrisy. The people do not know how to ask for what they really want; they only realize (too late) that it is not classroom experience. They are looking for something that they expect to encounter in the Bible but do not find on the face of it — perhaps to one sitting in the Adult Education committee meeting Wednesday night, the pastor's learned Bible study may seem as good a way as any to find it, but on Sunday morning the folly of that idea is painfully clear. What they want is not intellectual and cannot be satisfied by clever analysis. They are asking for something that will stimulate their devotion, in particular their love of the Bible. What they want is an object of love.

Preaching grace means presenting the biblical texts as objects of love. It involves telling the stories, arguing the arguments, living with the images. The preacher presents the texts which speak of God in hopes of seducing a people into a relationship with that God. As they fall in love with God, they fall in love with the texts, and vice-versa. Insofar as preaching instills this love, it is an act of grace, for love is a force from outside oneself.

As for the Bible study class, and the ongoing need for congregations to learn about these texts, this all takes place in due time. One does not study until one loves. People need to fall in love with texts before they will study them seriously. This is why I do not worry about parishioners seduced to God by fundamentalism. As they begin to grow, they will work their way up and through the nineteenth century. That is not so important in the beginning. What is important is that one learns to love God.

The preacher, too, learns to love God and the texts which reveal that God. This is why the preparation of a sermon, embracing both research and composition, is the ultimate devotional exercise. Here it is that the preacher has the experience of grace which will, God and the Spirit willing, be duplicated in the congregation on Sunday morning. The whole sermon process from start to finish is an act of worship and devotion, as the God encountered by the preacher in the biblical text is presented with those texts for the congregation's acclaim.

Paul told the Corinthians that "those who proclaim the gospel should live off of the gospel" (1 Corinthians 9:14, author's translation), by which he meant that preachers should draw paychecks. Paul's statement is unintentionally (?) profound, because not just our living but life itself proceeds from grace. We owe the day-to-day pains and joys of living — all that makes it worth getting up in the morning — to the sustaining gift of the One who put us here. This is never so true as in the pulpit — to preach is to rely on grace, because the preacher knows better than anyone that week after week the sermon begins with emptiness. There is nothing new or particularly important to say on Monday. Yet Sunday after Sunday, God gives something. The preacher knows that the sermon comes not from within but from without. One who stands in the pulpit has no choice but to live off of the gospel.

Once upon a time, a certain preacher bought a new car and took a long trip. The car ran fine, and the preacher rejoiced as the wheels hummed under his feet. The preacher was in fact so excited that he forgot that even new cars need gas. Too late he realized the needle was on empty. The car limped to the side of the interstate, far from an exit. The preacher had no choice but to get out and walk. The sun beat down on his head and withered the rest of whatever good mood he had left — if only he had not been so short-sighted and foolish!

A half-mile down the road, a dented red compact car pulled alongside the preacher. Inside was a big, burly, hairy bear of a man, the spitting image of everything mothers think of when they warn, "Don't talk to strangers." "You want a ride?" said the big man. "I hate to see people stuck on the freeway." The preacher stopped, looked at the big bear of a man, thought about his mother, looked down the long, empty, hot freeway, and decided it couldn't get any worse. "Sure," he said, and got in.

The big man, the compact car, and the preacher drove to the next exit, where the preacher bought a gas can and some gas. Then the man, the car, and the preacher drove back to the preacher's new car. All the while, the big friendly man entertained the preacher with stories about the salvation of stranded motorists. The man even helped the preacher, a mechanical klutz, pour the gas into the tank. Then the big, burly, hairy bear of a man and his little, dented red compact car drove away.

As the preacher waved his last good-bye and got back into his new car, he noticed a truck drive by. On one side of the truck was painted a single word, a company name, but much more: "Grace." It was.

Salvation always comes from the outside. Nowhere is this more true than with the preacher and the sermon. The preacher knows that each week the sermon begins with a Bible and a blank page, with nothing else but the hope that sometime during that week the preacher will encounter something from the outside, a word of grace. About five minutes before the Sunday service, or maybe on the second verse of the hymn, the preacher knows, usually in the pit of the stomach, that the sermon, though composed, cannot possibly be preached. Yet week by week, the page fills, the stomach lies down, and the mouth opens. By God's grace, the sermon comes.

1. Farley, "Preaching the Bible and Preaching the Gospel."

2. *Ibid.*, p. 93.

3. *Ibid.*, p. 97.

4. *Ibid.*

5. *Ibid.*, p. 100.

6. Fosdick, "Personal Counseling and Preaching," in Lischer, *Theories of Preaching*, p. 296.

7. Farley, "Preaching the Bible," p. 103.

8. An eloquent statement of the role of grace in the sermon, seen as attention to creation, judgment, and redemption, is William Muehl, *Why Preach? Why Listen?* (Philadelphia: Fortress Press, 1986).

www.ingramcontent.com/pod-product-compliance
Lightning Source LLC
Chambersburg PA
CBHW071723090426
42738CB00009B/1853